GOLD MAN REVIEW

Gold Man Review is published annually by Gold Man Publishing.

The editors invite submissions of previously unpublished works of fiction, nonfiction, and poetry. Manuscripts can be submitted at www.goldmanpublishing.com by following our submission guidelines.

Address all requests to:
Heather Cuthbertson
Editor-in-Chief
Heather.Cuthbertson@GoldManPublishing.com

Contents

Issue 9 Editor's Letter

This past year has been quiet. No births. No deaths. No fires[1]. Just the mundane day-to-day. I've welcomed it, but in the quiet, questions began surfacing in my consciousness. One of those had to do with an absolute truism so engrained in my identity I was surprised it was even on the table.

Am I a writer?

For nearly twenty years I've said I was one. I mean, I wrote a lot and chased the dream of publication, but I've never had any of my novels seen by anyone other than critique groups, agents, and editors in all that time. This last year I decided that was going to change.

I've had people suggest self-publishing to me in the past and, to be honest, I wasn't a fan. Not because I had anything against others who self-published, but it wasn't the dream I had for myself. I wanted to be traditionally published and all the trappings that went with it. Plus, when I first started writing, self-publishing had this stigma associated with it and that stuck with me even when the stigma had all but disappeared.

Then on New Year's Eve I was sitting on the couch, going through old novels I had written and walked away from—books I loved at the time and had been shopped to publishers but ended in a rejection pile. These files contained discarded years of my life. Then I figured, why not? Why not self-publish one of them? I'd changed direction as a writer and there was one, a young adult re-imagining of *Alice in Wonderland*, which would probably never see the light of day even if I did get my dream of traditional publishing. I stopped writing fantasy years ago and publishers tend to want writers to stick with the same genre, at least for a while.

That night, I committed to the idea and came up with a plan that emulated the methodology of traditionally published books. Thanks to *Gold Man Review*, I was already ahead of the game when it came to interior design and covers so my entire budget went to editing and marketing. After extensively editing for months and paying for two rounds of copy edits, it was ready. Equipped with an awesome cover and armed with a pen name, I paid for

---

[1] Sadly, I spoke too soon. Since initially writing this letter, fires have broken out in both Northern and Southern California.

three professional reviews (Kirkus, Clarion, and Foreword) and sent it on its way. Even if they hated it, all I needed was a decent blurb to get attention from reviewers, but luckily that wasn't the case. They were all great reviews and those professional reviewers gave me the confidence to take it to the next and final step: NetGalley.

Now if you've never heard of NetGalley, it is basically an online site where all kinds of reviewers—from the amateur to the professional—congregate. There is no vetting process to sign up as a reviewer (I did it) and it's free to do so. Publishers and self-publishers, on the other hand, pay a hefty fee to get their books on there, which I gladly did.

My expectations were minimal. I was hoping to get 100 review requests in the six-month period it was listed. That happened in 24 hours. When my listing ended, I had nearly 1800 reviewers who had requested to review my novel. At one point, it was the #1 Most Requested YA book in the UK and in the Top 5 Overall. In the US, it was one of the Top 5 Most Requested in YA and within the Top 10 Overall. This was all for this go-nowhere book that had sat in a file for almost ten years. It was doing so well NetGalley wanted to interview me. Not to sound cliché, but I was floating on cloud nine.

Then my cloud evaporated from underneath me. With all those requests came the reviews. I had great reviews (and still get them), but I also received not-so-great reviews. The 1-stars, 2-stars, and begrudgingly given 3-stars. That part of publishing rocked me to my core. Sure, I realized not everyone would like my book and it was unrealistic to expect nothing but glowing reviews, but what I hadn't anticipated was how much their words would affect me. I regretted publishing the book and was tempted to pull it. Even on the good days, the crippling self-doubt was ever-present. It was a difficult time for me, my family, and basically anyone around me. I didn't expect to take it so hard, but I suppose you never know how you're going to react until it happens to you.

The book was officially published August 1st and I've since emerged from this experience, I hope, better for it. It didn't completely rob me of my love of writing, although it came awfully close. It did, however, make me more hesitant to publish my work. There was a part to all of this I'd forgotten or ignored or just didn't realize would be a factor in my pursuit of publication: readers. I know how ridiculous that sounds. Writers and readers have an engrained symbiotic relationship, but after spending so many years trying and trying and trying to get published, I'd forgotten publishing was not about me, but about them. It's always for the readers. The critique group catch-all phrase, "Well, you see, what I was trying to do ..." doesn't fly when your words are available for download or purchase. You either resonated or you didn't and there's not a damn thing you can do about it. I'm sharing this experience so you don't make the same mistake I did. Remember the reader.

As of now, I'm currently revising an even older novel—the first one to get attention from a literary agent. It's a fantasy and I'm revising for me without any plans of publishing it. That's strange territory, but freeing. I have a newfound reverence for the courage and bravery it takes to engage in this art form. In our words is our hearts and souls, the truest expression of ourselves. Something so deeply personal it gets offered to the world with an almost child-like trust. Sometimes it is handled by others with the same amount of care. Sometimes it's chum in a pool of great whites. What matters is we continue to be a community. To be there for the writer who just had a bad review and the writer who had a great review. Or the writer who received a rejection in their email or one with an acceptance. These things are not mutually exclusive. It rains and shines on all writers and it's easy to feel very alone in the process, even to those with a solid support system. For me, I can't say what the next step is going to be. I'm taking it one sentence at a time, but my characters are always calling to me and, after almost twenty years, I couldn't ignore them even if I tried.

Until next year.

Sincerely,

Heather Cuthbertson
Editor-in-Chief
Gold Man Review

Gold Man Review Editors

The Old Man and The Speedo

jon bennett

He was an old man who swam alone in lane four of the Gulf Coast YMCA, and he had gone eighty-four days without taking a break.

During the first forty days, the boy politely acknowledged the old man when he saw him at swim practice. But after forty days, his companions on the swim team told him the old man was a creep, which is the worst kind of old man. So the boy ignored the old man's waves and allowed himself to be pulled into the swell of adolescent conformity.

The boy was the old man's neighbor, and he used to visit the old man regularly. He was in middle school then. The old man would sit on his front porch and rock in his sturdy oak chair, and the boy would ask the man questions about life, the universe, but mostly, about love. The boy's parents found his questions too uncomfortable to answer, so the boy turned to the well-dressed old man, who always stole a kiss from his wife when she brought him his afternoon mojito.

Sometimes the old man would lay in his hammock, swaying gently while humming a tune into his perspiring glass. The boy watched in admiration.

When the old man's wife passed away—a stroke, the boy was told—the old man lost the unshakeable confidence that comes from a life of good fortune. The old man no longer radiated. His clothes became threadbare. His slicked-back hair now tussled like a tangled white line. His back became humped, and his excess skin furled loose around his frame.

After four years of an empty bed and a vacant home, four years of quiet meals and silent rooms, four years of his body eating away its muscle and form, the old man decided to push back out into the world. He'd start simple. Revisiting the sport of his youth, he began swimming every morning eighty-four days ago.

The five a.m. crowd, a pack of waders, had drifted through most of their years. Many of the women had lost their significant others, either to death or dementia. In this lonely pool, the old man found he could finally angle for intimacy.

For the last eighty-four days, the old man laid out smiles and polite conversation without so much a nibble. It did not trouble him, though. Optimism pushed him into the waters every day. He just needed one good catch—just one person to ride out his last years with, now that his wife was gone, and the boy had drifted away.

The old man lowered himself from the steel gutters. A brief chill rose from his toes, to his knees, to his hips. His black speedo ballooned as the water trapped the air inside. He pressed his hands against the Spandex, setting off an eruption that bubbled against his back and belly. He smiled at Marin, the lifeguard, who gave a polite smile in return. She had worked at the pool for two years now. From the conversations Marin had with the old women, the old man could see a vague outline of her life swimming under the surface: increasingly independent teenage sons, a concern for coming college payments, a divorce. A series of life circumstances that chased her back to work.

Though distant in age, the old man had reeled her close through daily pleasantries and sociable gestures. He found romance floating in his thoughts, but he tried his hardest to fixate on the pursuance of friendship. He had found a companion, even if for only an hour and even if only at the pool. He did not want to scare her off.

The old man guided his goggles down from his forehead to his eyes and turned to the open pool in front of him. The straps cut against his ear, right at the place they connected to his head. His eyes bulged under the pressure of the plastic lenses he wore. But the old man counted them as worthy burdens to bear.

He submerged his body, feet floating up from the bottom until they found the painted concrete behind him. With a slight jump, he pushed out fully from the wall and coasted. Cold water crested the back of his head. His shadow tracked him along the black line on the bottom of the pool.

For twenty-five yards, his body rotated the same rhythmic motion: a toss of the arm then a spread of the hand, dragged through to catch as much water as possible. The other side mimicked the movements. He had honed an efficiency that developed since the first week.

Eighty-two days ago, Marin remarked how great the old man moved in the water, but that she was concerned his shoulders would hurt from over-reaching.

"How do I fix it?" the old man asked.

Marin demonstrated while standing next to him on the deck. She aligned her body as if she were floating horizontally in the pool.

"You want your arms to stay straight until you bend the elbows. Then pull along your ribs. You don't want your arm to come across your chest and belly."

She fluttered her legs to further pantomime the act of swimming. Her hips rippled gracefully, and her chest undulated. The old man smiled and nodded. Marin smiled in return.

"Thanks," the old man said. "I'll try it tomorrow."

"My pleasure."

The old man puffed his chest and moved to the locker room.

"Oh, I forgot to mention …" Marin's voice turned the old man "… the Makos will begin practicing in the water next week." She nodded her head at the high school swim team doing lunges around the pool. The boy trailed at the end of the line. His frail legs slowly bent his knee to the ground while the backs of the other boys crept further away.

In the three lanes next to the old man, a tempest rocked the channels where a school of boys thrashed. Triangles of bent elbows circled the lane, but the partition of plastic wheels strung from one wall to the other stood as a cage that kept them from the old man. Muted wake gently sloshed in and out of the old man's ears, dulling all but the voice inside his head. Today, like most days, Frank Sinatra crooned the old man's favorite tunes on repeat.

The old man took a breath. He tilted his head to the right. A blurry vision of Marin sat in her chair. The old man always felt that she watched him in particular. He returned his head to face down. His gradual exhale kept the water from stinging his nostrils. A slow string of pearls trickled from his nose. He lifted his head again to breathe the stagnant air. Marin, he thought, was definitely looking at him.

He touched the wall, rotated, and pushed back into the water. For the next twenty-five yards, he'd have to glance at the potbellied swim coach who always wore cargo shorts, even in the middle of winter. The coach never acknowledged the old man.

So it went for sixty more minutes until the dull pain in his shoulders and knees throbbed. The old man swam under a lane line and floated up to the surface like a manatee. He had to grab the line to steady himself. Once upright, he hobbled to the side, stealing glances of Marin as he trudged up the steps and out of the water.

"Had a good swim?"

The old man nodded. "It's always a good swim when you're on duty," he said.

Marin's teeth shimmered. She tucked loose strands of hair behind her ears, and her cheeks flushed.

"You're sweet."

"Same time tomorrow?" the old man asked.

"Of course," Marin replied with a smile.

The old man noticed his voice had deepened into a thick, smoky sweetness. He did not count this change as an embarrassment. Instead, a cloud of confidence covered him as he moved to the sauna, where the heat would loosen his joints.

The old man pulled the blue curtain to his shower. The light blue plastic flowed against the navy-blue cinderblock walls that encapsulated the old man. Just as warmth finally made its way from the shower, clangs of metal lockers echoed, and soon the squeaks of sandals approached. Boisterous voices from teenagers circled the old man's shower stall. He caught glimpses of skin through the slit between the curtain and the wall.

"Why you touching my butt, Bonnet?"

"If it bothers you, why you smiling so much, Tiger?"

A chorus of laughter rocked against the curtain. The man heard the boy's voice.

"You both are perverts."

"Speaking of creeps," Bonnet said somewhere in the mist. "Did you see that old man talking to my mom? Could practically see through his spee-do." A mixture of groans and chuckles rippled. "I bet if you looked close enough, you could see his saggy, wrinkled old-man balls."

More laughter.

"Bonnet, you probably did look close, and you probably liked it."

More laughter. A savage smack of a towel snapped repeatedly against a body. The old man sighed. He pulled the curtain closer to the wall and glanced down.

His fingers pinched the soggy, black fabric of his swimsuit. Its tautness had surrendered to time and chlorine. His hands crawled around the expanse of his waist. His right hand found a tear in the middle of his right butt-cheek. He fit two fingers through it.

How embarrassing, the old man thought, that Marin should see me like this.

He remained in the shower for thirty more minutes, enough time to let the ravenous boys race out into the dark morning, off to school where they'd find more damaged prey to appease their adolescent insecurities.

The old man hoped he'd find that the neighborhood boy had stayed back to give soft-hearted sympathy. But, of course, the boy had no way of knowing he was there. Instead of a friendly, familiar face, the old man only found wooden benches that carried the glean from damp towels and wet swimsuits. No other vestiges of humanity remained.

After his doctor's appointment, the old man went to the sporting goods store. A handful of college kids still on break rifled through the racks. They eyed the old man when he walked in from the white glow of the afternoon sun. Whispers and giggles swirled among the swimsuits and goggles.

The old man found the size markers bobbing above the speedos. He spotted his pant size. His flaccid pockets of skin would add an inch or so, he figured, but the tightness of the material would take it back. So he pulled a simple black suit, sans design or frill, shiny in its newness. Without trying it on, he paid the forty dollars and slipped out into the hot, stagnant air.

The next morning, the old man tugged on the top of the swimsuit. It clung to his thighs, barely surrendering an inch. The string around the waist cut into the flesh pockets on the old man's thumbs.

He bounced on his knees and wriggled his legs, moving the speedo two more inches with another three left to fully cover his bottom—its pale hills like scoops of vanilla ice cream or the backs of white elephants. His hands curled deeper into the fabric until he suddenly pulled out his left hand, which clenched like a claw.

"What is this," he said. "You choose to stop working now?"

The old man shook his hand. It remained frozen in defiance.

"Fine, I'll use the other hand."

He had to arch his back for the right hand to grasp the left side of his swimsuit—the side abandoned by his cramped left hand. A menacing thud bumped from the locker room door. Urgency spurred the old man to reign in his naked flesh. He wiggled and jumped some more. Before the teen saw him, the old man coerced his lycra net to rest high enough near his hip that he could feel comfortable with its coverage. He draped his towel around his neck and slammed his locker shut.

The old man pinched his goggles in his only functioning hand and shoved out to the pool deck—body enveloped by bright white rays of florescent light. Marin welcomed the old man's emergence with a smile.

"New suit?"

The old man nodded.

"Have to look my best." He winked.

Marin's cheeks flushed.

"Well, the suit looks good," she said.

The old man blushed in return, forgetting the subversive cramping of his hand. He walked to the steps and lowered himself into the pool, resting his clenched hand on a bed of warm water. He moved to the wall, hand skimming the water at his waist.

For the first five laps, he floundered on his side. His right arm dragged the entirety of his weight while his left arm limped through the water due to the broken blade at the end of it. The old man's shoulder began to ache twenty minutes before it should have.

The surge from the swim team rocked the old man's body. Just moving forward became an arduous task. He battled the current and the stabbing pain in his shoulders. For the first time, the old man thought about ending his workout after only fifteen minutes, but the cloudy vision of Marin swam beside him with each breath he took. He could not quit now. What would Marin think? What would Sinatra do?

The old man caught a glimpse of the neighbor boy standing at the wall. Legs and arms splashed around him, leaving a wake in their path. The old man wasn't sure, but he thought the boy gave a tight nod of acknowledgment and a small, tense smile. A twinge of guilt racked the old man for even thinking about quitting.

The old man propelled off the wall and continued his swim. His feet trailed his body more like an anchor holding him back than a motor pushing him forward. Still, he pulled and pulled and pulled at the invisible line that hauled him from one end to the other. His back tightened. His muscles clamped around his spine. His knees throbbed with an icy knocking.

His neck tugged at his shoulder blades. All the while, golden slivers of light swirled around Marin.

When the hour ended and the old man's hand hit the cold metal gutter, he turned his bow to the steps. His chest heaved, and he staggered with the first steps, but he maintained his smile. Marin watched him.

"You had quite a workout today."

"I sure did. Felt great," the old man said. He winced, however, as he noticed a weight sitting heavy on his chest

"I bet. I would swim after my shift, but I forgot my suit."

"That's a shame. I guess you'll have to get coffee instead."

Marin smirked. "Oh yeah?"

"Just a cup. It's on me."

Marin chuckled and nodded. "Ok."

She peered around the old man quickly, scanning the high school swim team, which was wrapping up practice.

The old man's chest fluttered through the thick fog. He tied her acceptance to his heart and sailed off to the bathroom. The heaviness of his exercise did not nag him while he sat buoyantly in the sauna and shower. The pain that drifted down his arm could not quiet the joyful whistle he sang into his clothes. He practically danced to the door before realizing he hadn't shored up the time and location. He moved back to the pool deck, where three of the high school boys encircled Marin.

"Mom, you're getting coffee with him? He's a creep."

"Yeah, Ms. B, he was talking to himself while he got into his bathing suit. I heard him when I went to the bathroom."

"Did you see how tight that thing was? You could practically see his shriveled old man parts."

The boys burst into laughter. Marin stared silently at her hands. The old man saw the boy standing a few feet away. The boy's face did not mirror the sardonic enthusiasm of the others. He covered his head with the towel and rubbed it forcefully against his scalp.

"He's sweet," Marin said.

"He's a creep," her son repeated.

"Yeah, Ms. B, you don't want to be alone with him," another boy said.

"I don't know," Marin whispered, "I told him I'd go." She stared at the holes in the red lifeguard tube laid across her lap. Her fingers scraped out chunks of yellow foam. "It's not romantic or anything. I think he just wants a friend."

"It's okay. He's probably got to get back to his nursing home. Probably missing Bingo or something," her son said. He bared his teeth. "We can get breakfast instead. I'll tell dad not to pick me up."

Marin glanced up at him. Her eyes twitched, hooked by the opportunity her son laid out.

"Okay," she whispered, "I'll just tell him something came up."

But she never got a chance to tell the old man. He dove quickly back to the locker room. Rejection afflicted him. It chased him home with such haste that he didn't notice his speedo had fallen to the floor.

In the car, he couldn't distinguish his disappointment from his countless other aches, including the clenching around his heart. When he brushed past the hammock on his front porch, a surge of tightness wrapped around his neck. He staggered into his house and turned to close the door. But he only succeeded in pushing it far enough so that a sliver of the morning sun sliced through the table in his entry.

Fear, dejection, hopelessness, all the shadowy shapes of his house that he hadn't seen in eighty-five days, encircled him. He stumbled to his reprieve—his old record player—flicked it on, and, with shaking hands, guided the needle to its place on the spinning record.

The old man lowered himself on the tan cushions of his couch, man and furniture groaning together. He laid his head on the pillow, hoisted up his feet, and crossed his arms—surrendering himself to the sweet sounds of his favorite song, which played him out to sea.

The boy found the old man's speedo. To his parents' surprise and pride, the boy adamantly demanded they take him home so that he could return the swimsuit before school. He could be late for homeroom, he argued.

The car pulled up the old man's driveway. From the front seat, the boy's parents watched their son sprint to the porch, where the old man's door yielded to the boy's knocking. The boy peered into the house. He inched part the frame, then disappeared, but only for a minute.

The boy spilled back into the morning sun, mouth agape and lips trembling, hands gripping the tiny black swimsuit as if it was life itself.

poem

Irritable Bowel

leah mueller

No matter what diet
you decide to eat,
you're going to die.
The question is: how soon?

What parts of self
would you care to sacrifice
to get to your destination?

Your shoulders,
knees and pancreas,
all are ripe for the taking.

It's not just food:
your diet includes everything
you see and hear:

the homeless man on the corner
with his misspelled cardboard sign
announcing he's hungry.

The braying voice on the radio
condemning the new regime.
The sound of static overhead
as war planes do their practice runs.

The line of cars
by the freeway onramp,
waiting to be eaten alive.

You take it all inside your body,
mix the bundle
with saliva and tears,
digest it like carpet tacks
and sour milk, try your best
to expel what you can't use.

If you get ill, it's
your own goddamn fault:

you'd better just keep swallowing,
and remember to mix
your moral outrage
with plenty of extra fiber.

Memory

barbara mcclure

The thing I most remember about the house was the first time I tried heroin. That and the house itself, a two-story, rather square, that sat at the back of the lot, apart from the normal row of houses on both sides. Why it was set off like this I never thought about until now. It was a small house even though it had two bedrooms upstairs at the end of a narrow staircase, a box-like structure like one of those buildings used for fire training. In the entry was a tiny sitting room with a Persian rug, ferns on matching wooden plant stands, framing an antique writing desk, all bought from an estate sale of an elderly woman whose family was moving her into a nursing home. Strange that neither of us ever used this room. In the living room sat an old upright piano, a couch with a thin Madras bedspread over it to cover the sagging, worn-out cushions, an amp, a drum set, a music stand, and a few unmatched wooden chairs. This was where the band practiced, where I spent little time. A small, narrow kitchen sat behind the music room and in the pantry off the kitchen is where my Irish Setter gave birth to four large Great Dane-sired pups. The Dane belonged to him.

These are the rooms I remember, like aged black and white Polaroids tacked up inside my brain. I remember walking into the house, seeing the plants on the right and the piano on my left and going up those stairs, the bedroom being my refuge. That's the memory: a July summer night in Wichita.

Over forty years later I picture this home, my ex now long dead of pancreatic cancer, long after we'd split up. I am sitting in a fishing lodge outside of Craig, Montana, in this small, dark room where my husband and I have returned from an afternoon engagement party on the Missouri River. No one else is here at the lodge yet, no other guests, no manager, just the two of us and two deer that graze on the hill behind the building. The owner left the key in the doorknob and put us in room six in the back, facing the foothills of the mountain. The only channel on the small flat screen is ESPN and it's fight night. We turn it on just as the first fight has ended, and a bloodied, light-brown face grins as someone pulls up his gloved fist in victory, the announcers excitedly reviewing the fight, highlighting the fact that their suits are splattered with blood. Until this night I have never watched an evening of boxing on TV. I've never watched a fight, period. Now I have watched three fights in a row. I have no idea what triggers the memory of the Wichita house, the night I tried heroin. A decade later, it bothers me.

The July heat in Wichita presses against the walls as if moving them in, making everything smaller, claustrophobic. A revolving fan sits on the old wood floor in front of the open window upstairs, turned off, where I sit against a wall, snorting through the cutoff straw the lines of heroin Larry drew on the glass, rectangular tray. Larry is my ex's friend, a lead-guitar player, a new dad with a woman he'll later split up with and never marry. He'd brought the heroin for us to try.

"How do you feel?" he asks.

"Nothing," I reply. He offers me a couple more lines, but I shake my head no and stay leaned against the wall.

Larry leaves just before the ten o'clock news, and we are getting into bed to watch the TV that sits balanced on the dresser when the phone rings. I hear my ex say, "Hang on," and he pulls the black phone cord outside the bedroom, partially closing the door so all I can hear is a muffled whisper mixed with the local anchor's too shrill voice. I am sitting on top of the still-made bed in my underwear and a t-shirt, my knees hugging my chest, trying to decide if I'm high off the heroin. I feel something. Maybe tired. Maybe down.

In Montana the blue birds like to perch on top of the newly planted spruce, one singing to another nearby bird who replies. I watch from inside my kitchen window when I suddenly hear the chirping of ospreys and run to the deck to see them above me, their spread wings revealing the beautiful snowy-colored breasts, the sun lighting up the golden brown through the spread wings, the pair of them, circling, mates for life. This is what happens in Montana in the morning: the quiet, the solitude, the moment of unexpected beauty. I wonder how old I will be when these will become nothing but memories.

When he comes back into the room, I notice that he's left the phone out in the hall. I have turned on the small lamp next to the bed and wait for him to speak first. He pulls up his jeans, zipping them and reaches for his t-shirt.

I press the mute button on the remote. "If you go to her tonight, don't come back."

For a long time, he says nothing, his back to me. He hesitates and then slowly pulls on his t-shirt over his head, slipping his arms through with little effort, not looking at me. He slowly fastens his wristwatch, everything in slow motion, as if weighing his options.

When I was young, I remember going fishing with my father somewhere outside of Wichita. He had an old Folgers coffee can, filled with dirt where he kept his worms. He'd tease me as he'd pull a squirming one out. "Want to put it on for me?" I'd wrinkle my nose, shake my head, and back away as he'd weave it onto the hook, spit on it, and throw the line into the dark pond water, the red and white bobber floating on top. "Watch closely and when you see the bobber go under, lift up the pole." He handed me the rod and I offered him his cold can of Pabst. I would stare at the bobber until my eyes burned as if I were locked into a staring contest. I didn't want to fail.

I remember our next-door neighbor, the father of a child I used to color with, coming home from work in his suit. He had a black mustache and black hair. Maybe he was from India? He would tell us funny stories that almost seemed true to a five-year-old, something about the parade of elephants on the street where he worked. I remember our boxer when my father put up the electric fence that would keep the dog from escaping the backyard. I remember the first time I smoked pot outside the Wichita city limits in Logan Anderson's VW bug. I remember the ceramic donkeys on the restaurant lawn on the way to the Oakland airport. I remember the peach-colored print dress I wore at my birthday party when I got the new pink bicycle and stood for a picture, a coat slightly hiding the new dress, surrounded by my three best friends. Or is it the photograph that I remember? I remember driving down 13th Street in the backseat of my dad's car, seeing a man about to push a woman out the third-floor apartment window of a brick building. I was told I was imagining things as my father drove around the block and passing by the building again, all we saw was the brick building, no woman.

He sits down at the end of the bed. I do nothing but watch. He removes his watch and sets it on the dresser, slides off the jeans, pulls down the bed covers and slips in beside me, turning his back to me—all seemingly in one, fluid, slow motion. I lean over and shut off the light on the nightstand and stay seated, hugging my knees in the dark. I can't sleep. The news now over, Johnny Carson appears, and I increase the volume, just as a commercial comes on. I switch off the TV and the light, and through the open window I see the nearly full moon as it seems to be rising higher, try to make out the rabbit shape I remember the child pointing out to me when I was standing in line for tacos in Santa Barbara one summer during the Spanish Fiesta, the taqueria made famous by Julia Child. The phone that is still pulled out into the hallway rings, its muffled sound like a wakeup call, urgent, unending. He remains motionless next me though I know he's not yet sleeping.

In Montana when we fish the Madison River, we practice patience. First, there is the ritual of getting ready to fish, setting up the rods, putting on the waders, spraying on sunscreen and bug repellant, giving an offering of tobacco at the river with prayer. The geese with six goslings float in and out of the bank willows nearby. Caddis rise in clouds around us, but we don't see rising fish. Still, we cast, change the fly, cover a lot of water, and keep casting. Again, I am carefully watching the water.

poem

Abadania

rachel barton

In Abadania, we dress in white when we go to the Casa.
We sit in a current of mediation as scores of broken people
file past us for the fathers' healing.
Later, at the *pousada*, I leave my fish bones on the plate
to walk between the market stalls
where two boys zip by on a moped, laughing.

Before sunset I find Regina, infant at her breast,
selling the instruments and jewelry of her mountain tribe.
I purchase wooden whistles scored with burnt wood designs
and two bracelets of bleached-porcupine-vertebrae-
and-black-onyx which she blesses in her broken English--
Courage, strong heart, she says. *My people protect you.*

The sky is radiant with tongues of fire.
Soon it will grow dark and fill with the trace of spirits--
orbs of many sizes we can see through our camera lenses.
I will stand beneath a waterfall and shiver, I will lie under
an array of crystals. And one evening, after my surgery,
my guide will appear to me, blue as Krishna, and tell me
it is time to come Home.

nonfiction

On Orogenies
savanna ferguson

Orogeny: A mountain building event, especially a mountain building event in history.

Please know I wasn't drawn to geology because of you. You drew me in because of geology. It's a problem of mine, attraction to those who love what I love, instead of those who might love me. A subject/object conflation.

You understood the way geology mixed my love of landscape with my love of language: *oolite, igneous, Silurian, serpentine, batholith, xenolith, Carboniferous, calcification, moraine, ultramafic, horst and graben.* This poetry of description. It was after "us" that I learned *orogeny.* But I feel you in that word. I feel us. *Orogeny, orogenesis, orogenic.* Orogeny: or–*Ahh*–jenny. A round word to wrap around a smooth tongue, soft in all its dimensions, but so powerful in its meaning: building mountains, *Orogeny. Oro* for the Greek "mountain," *geny*—to create, to form. Orogeny, the sounds so close and yet so far from erogeny—erogenous. Mountains in the earth, mountains in the body.

Bedrock: The Sawtooth Batholith
The Sawtooth Mountains of central Idaho are cut like jagged scythes, the color of lips, the texture of broken bone. They were carved by earthquake and weather from an isolated pool of pink granite known as the Sawtooth Batholith. The mountains are surrounded by the gray granite of the much larger Idaho Batholith—the cooled remnants of a long past volcanic history. The Sawtooths carve the skyline over Stanley Basin.

I spent a week in those mountains, months after you and I. The water was cold; the lakes were deep. The ridges shone in the sun like the heart of a rose. From the slopes you can see across the Stanley Basin to the east. In that part of Idaho, the winters run cold and wet. The summers burn hot and dry. There are heavy winds and electrical storms.

The mountains' plants are few, nothing like the Appalachia I knew so well, or the Boundary Waters you knew. There are lodgepole pines and sage, a few wildflowers. But they are enough to tell a story. The places where the pines turn to sage intimate changes in the soil and therefore changes in the rock beneath. They're clues, signs on the surface of boundaries below.

There is so much that happened before the beginning, and the end was hardly an ending, since I am still within this. I want to tell, but I also want to hold back, keep something for myself, enough to let go without losing.

I think these two orogenies are palm-to-palm. Subject reflected in object. Two breeds of volcanic upwelling.

We met through coincidence my first week in college. You'd had my dorm room the year before. When I moved in, the first message I received on the phone was for you: "Gabriel, this is your father. Please call me. You can reach me at work tomorrow. I'm not sure if this is still Gabriel's number. If it isn't, would somebody please find Gabriel Devin and tell him to call his father?" The man's voice was deep and direct, like yours, but gruffer.

In my first few days at college, I hardly knew how to find my classrooms, let alone one individual out of hundreds of students. I thought the request so absurd, I told my first friend in college. My warp and your weft were in Fate's loom. Ben, my first, my only friend on campus, knew you from camp in Minnesota.

The next morning, the first day of classes, Ben pointed you out to me on our way to introductory geology. My backpack was slung awkwardly in front of me as I searched in its pockets, and my hair, wet from the shower, hung over my face. I tossed my head back and called out to this tall, slender boy with long blond hair standing twenty paces away in the grass of the main lawn.

"Gabriel Devin?" You looked in my direction, and I was suddenly aware of my backpack and soggy hair. "Your dad called, and he would like you to call him back. You can reach him at work."

"Oh, thanks," was all you said. You didn't know who I was or how I had gotten the message. You didn't seem to care. So I walked away and learned of plate tectonics, continents moving across the globe—collisions and driftings apart.

We saw little of one another that first semester. At some point we were formally introduced, and soon enough the year progressed, and the warm, dry days turned into a brisk autumn, until finally winter arrived: cloudy, gray, and bitterly cold. In eastern Washington, a supposed desert, it seemed always to be raining. January and February were the same through and through. No colder than my Virginia winters, but without a drop of snow to capture the light. My hands and feet grew pale and frigid, and I watched as freezing fog built spikes of ice crystals on fences and the limbs of trees. It wasn't until the first hints of spring, of blossoms, that you and I moved beyond passing hellos.

There are things made right by the spring—trees, streams, the color of the sky—and there are other things that can only be right in the spring. Colors, always pastels. They are strands of silk, intertwined with sentimentality, delicate and strong, a spider net. The urgency of the flowers seeped into my eyes and pores and crept along my nerves. The warmth in the light and the cool of the shade were blankets, pillows, blinders. A lilac breeze that lifts the weight of winter. I rushed in, my heart in my teeth, lust lain flat against the palm of my hand. I was April's fool.

The granite of the Sawtooth Batholith is pink like that spring. Of all the mountains I've ever seen, I recall no contrast more striking than that of the Sawtooth's bloom beside the winter gray of the Idaho Batholith. While both granite, slight differences in age and minerals alter their hues even though the Sawtooth's stone comes from the Idaho. The granite of the Sawtooths is twenty million years younger than the gray granite surrounding it. It's new, geologically speaking, fresh, that's partly why the peaks are so sharp. The Sawtooth Batholith formed from a partial melting of the Idaho Batholith, welling up from magma deep beneath the continent during the Tertiary period. The crystals in the rocks are also smaller than those of the Idaho Batholith because they were given little time to form. They would have grown, given more time. The Sawtooth granite cooled rapidly in its shallow placement just below the surface.

It began for you, I believe, with a tempered discussion on a cool Sunday afternoon. The world outside the bay window was crisp and sunny, but the world we nine discussed inside was filled with rage, with an imminent war and a corruption of politics that could break you. I thought I spoke too much. I was pained, but more, I was well-informed. It only made me angrier, more verbose. There was something in my words that struck you, though I've never asked what that something was.

You became suddenly friendlier, more inclined to approach me in the library, at dinner, when I crossed campus. You would look at me with those crystalline blue eyes, their darkened centers always so wide when they fell on me. There was a smirk in your eyes and lifted note in your greetings. In your Minnesota flatness, the change of tone was more than obvious. When we sat together, the smooth muscles of your forearms stretched across the table between us. I remember your hands, slender, knuckles contouring each finger, hands that fixed bikes and ran down my arms in greeting. The gaps between your teeth brought a softness to your smiles. But there was a spark, too, like electricity before a thunderstorm.

I was drawn to you like I am drawn to landscape. Your body was some kind of foreign terrain. Taut and smooth beneath old t-shirts and plaid button-ups, straight leg jeans and corduroys. Your movements were catlike, a slightly effeminate gate, a consistent *contre-posto* stance like Michelangelo's "David." Your skin a golden sheen, and not even the faintest mustache. This is how I saw you.

You floated through conversations, rarely asking for information, often coming off as the quieter of your friends, only supplying that which was requested.

Before the Sawtooths formed, Idaho's tectonic plate, its continental shelf, was compressed east to west for millions of years, deforming the rocks and building tension within the folds like the tight coils of a spring.

Some part of me has swallowed whole the moment I knew you wanted me, sitting on the brown velour couch in your dorm room, waiting to start a movie. The moment you brought the thin quilt your grandmother made over to the couch and tucked it discreetly over both our legs. I took that knowing and buried it in the soft of my abdomen, tucked it under my ribs.

We are so reliant on our vision that the things we do beyond sight can be questioned. This is why, of course, I brushed the inside of your forearm beneath the blanket and you, in turn, brushed the inside of my thigh. Yet, when your arm came out from under the blanket and wrapped over my shoulder, it couldn't be unseen. I remember nothing of the film.

I had to kiss you, an unfortunate necessity of my more daring nature, or perhaps your timidity, or perhaps your pride. It seems almost ridiculous now, to think back and say that I was, after all, the braver. What does it say about a boy who has never been the one left behind? Who has always broken up with the girl, but never moved in for the first kiss?

Once the movie ended, we made small talk regarding the map of the U.S. pinned to the wall above the couch. I was still sitting, my legs tucked under me, and you, you stood, though almost kneeling, your knees pressed into the edge of the couch. You traced your fingers along the Boundary Waters. I traced Appalachia. Showing each the other's known landscapes, our bodies their own boundary waters and mountain chains, just inches—miles—between us. And the rift, continental, might have survived, but that I turned to you, waited for that moment when I lost interest in your words for watching your lips move. I pushed myself up from the couch, kneeling towards your half-kneeling figure.

Do you remember what you said to me afterwards? You said, "Way to be assertive."

The very first kiss was awkward. It wasn't magical or perfect. It was only a moment of recognition. It was second and third and umpteenth kisses that arced down my throat and took hold of the muscles between my ribs, those kisses that sent electric pulses into my spine, across my arched shoulders, wrapping around my heart's memory.

When the compression finally stopped, the continental shelf began to expand, releasing the spring, rifting, but rocks do not stretch and lay flat as the buildup is satisfied, the tension released. They break, they fault, allowing one side to move upward and the other to drop below. Throughout Idaho the landscape became littered with mountains and valleys. Geologists refer to the mountain and valley systems formed by rifting as horst and graben complexes.

I know you remember touching the map. We didn't point to the Sawtooths. I didn't know them then. I don't know if you ever have.

We took long walks through the neighborhoods of our college town on cool spring evenings awash with lilacs, cherry blossoms, and dogwoods. We discussed the war, Nietzsche's thoughts on punishment, and the blight of the American chestnut. I identified trees, you told me about the formation of the Canyonlands in Utah, of the flat expanses in the Great Lakes. You told me you struggled with every paper you wrote, would give your world to write with confidence. You told me geology simply made sense to you. It was clear and concise. You understood it as you understood chemistry and the mechanics of a bicycle, things I failed to grasp. You were a geology major. I was a geology minor, but you, like me, truly wanted to be a naturalist. A naturalist wishes to hold the knowledge of the world within the space of the body, to all at once be at home in and to be the home of the tangible world.

You wished sometimes to escape from the inaction of academia, simply to go out and get in up to your elbows. As our relationship grew, I learned that you wanted a job that would sit easy on your morals. You would not allow yourself to be dragged into the destructive careers of so many geologists. These proclamations came without consideration for their effect on me, but my heart pressed against my sternum, reaching for you.

We fell into an unspoken routine. We would work in the library until eleven or twelve at night. It was a give and take; you would wait for me sometimes, but more often, I would wait for you. We would gather our things and bike three blocks to your dorm. You never once stayed in my room with me. You taught me how to ride my bike without hands. A risk, a freedom. You taught me how to let go without falling.

We would get ready for bed together, brushing our teeth at the sink in your room, a remnant from the dorm's former life as a hospital. Sometimes we would sit for a while beforehand and talk. We always had to wait for your roommate, Neil, to come in and gather his own things so he could spend the night with his girlfriend across campus. Sometimes there were other people in the room too, seated on the couch, the two desk chairs, or the lower bunk. Sometimes they lingered and chatted, played Neil's guitar, or talked with you. Sometimes they talked with me, but those conversations were limited. Their eyes slid over me in question. They didn't know me; didn't know how you had come to know me. Didn't know why Gabriel, unattached but admired for his first year and a half at college, had chosen this girl. If I knew why, perhaps it wouldn't hurt so much. But I didn't know, and I don't know, and I don't want to ask you now.

Sometimes the uncertainty of your friends crept in and made me question your choice of me. I felt undeservedly lucky, which is of course why it wasn't love. Falling in love with another person makes you fall in love with yourself.

What I loved was our routine. I loved that I had a toothbrush all my own in your room. I hated scrambling up to the top bunk, climbing over Neil's computer and the slats at the foot-end, but I loved curling myself into those sheets and quilts. I loved your body wrapped against me. I slept against the wall. Beside me, you rolled onto your right side, left arm thrown across my chest, right arm tucked between us. You curled your knees up under my legs and I felt your every breath against my shoulder, felt your muscles twitching before you fell asleep.

Cenozoic Faulting

It seems improbable, but kissing you felt like letting go, instead of holding on. Like leaping off a rock into an alpine lake. There was a pulse that passed between us and I wanted it to become a rhythm.

When we were first together, we had long conversations before falling asleep. Twice we distanced ourselves enough to talk about relationships. The first time you told me, "Well, I suppose the grass is always greener on the other side. When I'm single, I want to be in a relationship, and when I'm in a relationship, I want to be single. I mean, when I'm alone it's great at first, and then, then I get tired of it. It's the same when I'm with someone."

"Well, how do you feel right now?" I asked, cheek resting against your shoulder.

"Oh, now?" You laughed a little. "This is good." Your laugh was awkward, always, a guttural guffaw. I suspect you were startled by the question. You never thought to screen your words according to your audience. I was your confidant, not a girlfriend. You were honest to a fault.

We would have made great friends.

The fault that resulted in the formation of the Sawtooths occurred when the crustal block, this hardened pool of granite, divided. The western block lifted, invisibly buoyed, to birth the Sawtooth Range. In the east, the crustal block dropped down to form the Stanley Basin. The Sawtooths rose, sheer blocks of granite: naked, solid, exposed.

Things became shaky weeks before they ended between us. I have page after page of journal entry to attest to the fact.

We did have our moments, but they were too few, too far between to sustain us. I remember one particular night. It was a night in which we let go, a little, of who we were. It was a dance, a cross-dressing affair. I wore your suit pants; they were a little too long and tucked under my heels. You wore a black satin slip, a wig, some makeup I had artfully applied. I hadn't known until that night that your eyelashes were so very long. They were so light they had been almost invisible before.

I wore a business shirt and suspenders. My hair was high on the top of my head in a ponytail, the dark curls rolling down my neck. I danced like I was both myself, the girl, and in these clothes, the man. I was rhythm and lust and the way we touched on the dance floor—it had never been like that before. You weren't afraid to touch me in the middle of that crowd, to claim that I was yours. I remember late in the evening you quickly ran your hand up the inside of my leg, pressed between my thighs and whispered, "My, well, you're not a boy."

You were so wonderfully strange that night, freed from the constraints of reputation by wearing a skirt. Perhaps we need to escape ourselves to become our desires.

You were not with me, but on my first night in the Sawtooths, just a few months after us, there was a thunderstorm. The sky turned—lightness to lead. The storm came early in the evening, and I sat beneath the shelter as the ground became a lake, reassuring my companions, counting the time between the flashes of lightning and the claps of thunder. The gravel and pine needles beneath my boots grew damp and loose, and wind whistled through slits in the tarp. I have lived through a thousand storms in Appalachia. I am cautious of lightning, but I am not afraid of it. I counted the strikes from eight miles away in the west until the bolts were right upon us, simultaneous flashes and explosions. I counted until they were eight miles away in the east.

In the middle of the storm we had to move our shelter. What had appeared to be flat ground in the afternoon had quickly dissolved into rivers and swamps. We settled before dark on the slanted ground a hundred feet from the deep blue waters of Toxaway Lake. I woke a dozen times to pull myself up from the foot of the shelter, dragging my sleeping pad across the damp base of the tent, hoping my feet would not begin to feel the water seeping through my sleeping bag.

The next morning was bright and clear. We spread our belongings across the granite outcroppings to dry in the sun. There was not a drop of rain for the next five days we were there, as if the storm had never been.

We were sleeping together but had not slept together. On the couch, your room, some Saturday night, I wound up naked on my belly, draped across you like a throw. You, still in your jeans, your shirt only unbuttoned.

"How do you feel about sex?" you asked.

"I feel good," I said. You smiled. I remember moonlight through the hospital window. It was late. I put on pajamas. We climbed to bed.

A week later, we talked about relationships for the second time. We did not talk about our own relationship, directly that is. We were, of course, talking about you and me all along, but neither would admit it. We sat on either end of that velour couch in your converted-hospital dorm room. You told me that, for you, relationships ended up being compromises, that you couldn't imagine committing to compromise right now. I told you that once or twice in my life I had met a man I thought I could be with always, but that I regretted meeting them so young. I didn't think, I said, a relationship so young could last. You looked at me from your corner of the couch, head tilted, the light from Neil's desk lamp casting shadows across your face. "Well, who's to say that you couldn't meet again in a few years and have it work?" Were you thinking of yourself?

Neil knocked, and you got up to let him in. When he entered, our conversation ended, but I sat stiffly on the couch, my arms crossed, hands hidden. You sat back on the couch and pulled my feet into your lap, rubbing my soles with your strong thumbs. Neil chatted, put some books on the desk, and abandoned us.

When we crawled into bed, you lay on your back and I rolled toward you. I needed to know what was going to happen when we left for the summer. I couldn't hold back anymore. You said, "I'm tired. We'll talk about it tomorrow night, OK?"

"OK," I whispered.

Within minutes you were asleep. You rolled away from me and pushed towards the wall, against my still body. The space grew tight. As carefully as I could, I sat up, crawled down from the bed, and curled on the couch with your extra quilt. I curled myself tightly into the brown velour and let the tears come in quiet spasms. I didn't have the nerve to leave.

When the alarm went off the next morning you were surprised to see me on the couch. "What are you doing over there?" you asked, turning to me from the bunk.

"You kind of squished me out," I said, pushing myself up to a sitting position.

"Oh," you said, your cheek against the edge of the mattress, "I didn't even notice you were gone."

Pleistocene Glaciation

There were three periods of intensive glaciation that came to shape the Sawtooths. The smooth valleys curved from one peak to the next like the path of a pendulum is the first piece of evidence. The serrated ridges came from frost wedging into and breaking the flesh-toned granite.

I was stranded on a suburban lawn in eastern Washington on a cold evening, May fifth. My heart felt slow. I sat on the slope of the lawn, my legs bent, my arms wrapped around them, hands clasped, head down. I had spent hours crying, for you, for myself, for the question I couldn't answer. Where is the fault, the fracture that presaged this collapse?

We had not gone to your room, or to the library, our routine for weeks now. We took a walk, like we had in the beginning, though the beginning was just a few weeks past.

"I know most people just have emotions," you said, sitting a few feet to my left, reclined against your backpack on the damp grass, ankles crossed, hands in your pockets. Both of us faced the sidewalk and street. "I know most people don't have to think about a situation before they know how they feel about it, but, well, I'm not like that. I hadn't really thought about how I feel until today. I thought about it a lot, and I just realized, this isn't working for me."

I was calm, almost sedate, accepting of the moment. I feigned agreement. I did not protest or argue. The air, the grass, was wet and soaking into my clothing. I did not cry. The tears were all around me.

There are other telltale signs of the glaciation at the base of the range, piles of debris in moraines, cirques; there are glacier-polished rock outcroppings. The Sawtooths, though, do not preserve much of their erosional history; the rocks are simply bare, clean—as if nothing has changed.

The topography, the landscape that I soaked in there was created by the work from those glaciers. The mountains' beauty came after the Sawtooths were built by faults. You must understand: the Sawtooths are striking because they eroded. Because of Pleistocene ice flows, sun, rain, and violent winds.

I was suspended in ache for a few months' worth of moments that added up to nothing. Only I ever saw the mountains, ever traced the glaciated ridge. Caught in nothing more than moments, a pastel spider's web, lightness and lead. You are not the one. But my heart sits in the curl of my stomach, unyielding. The stomach-heart leaps every time you approach. My God, the stomach-heart is foolish.

Orogeny isn't always easy to discern. Evidence for the tectonic origin of the Sawtooth Mountains is limited to the linearity of the range, the magnetic patterns of the underlying rock, and the mountains' similarity with other horst and graben features in the Rocky Mountains. The one telltale sign, the fault scarps, the scarred margins of the rock along the fault boundary of any range borne of tectonic rift, are not evident. They have been concealed by more recent geologic events, mostly waste from the glaciers. You can see the mountains alongside the valley, they are a stony anomaly in the otherwise green landscape, but you cannot see the break between the valley and the mountain. You cannot perceive the fault.

You are not the problem. And perhaps neither am I. It is the combination. Of time and spring, of an upwelling that grew and then cooled too quickly. A raw, pink scar obscured.

On the day we left the Sawtooths, I hiked the last mile alone. I crunched the stones beneath my feet and breathed the cool air deep into my lungs. I pulled you up from the rocks and in. The gravel grinding against the soles of my boots, the weight of each step tightening the muscles of my thighs. Breathing. The weight of my pack, heavy and firm, a rhythm in my shoulders, pressing on my hips. You on the bed indifferent to my absence. You on a lawn, indifferent to my ache. You kissing me, you against my body, part of my body, knowing, no, not quite, all of my body. Am I grateful? Grit and gravel, descent. I breathed in and in. The trail levels. Breathe out.

The Sawtooths are shaped still by gentle processes: frost wedging, rock falls, talus and soil creep, stream erosion, rock-glacial flow. The effects of the glaciers today are minor in comparison to the Pleistocene events.

When I see you now, we sometimes talk for hours. I confessed to you once, "I was worried you wouldn't want to talk to me."

"Who could resist?" You said and smiled, just slightly.

I am no longer at risk of losing you.

You know better than I, that to be precise with geological terminology, the series of faults that formed the Sawtooths are not technically orogenies. The term orogeny, while general in its definition, a mountain building event, is used by experts only in reference to collisional tectonism, the compression of one continental plate with another. By this constraint, orogenies occur when the plates push and fuse and fold together, not when they move apart without affecting the shape of the other.

But they are mountains, and I felt the collision. One's shape affected by another.

The Man in My Attic

j.t. townley

Got a man in my attic. Come home late from Our Lady of Grace, and he's moved in, lock, stock, and barrel. Course, I don't notice at first. That's a lie, an untruth, it ain't quite the whole story. I don't put two and two together. I flop onto my bedroll and take a long swill of elixir, letting that fire warm me from the inside out, then set myself to singing. Just open my maw and let the melody flow:

Ain't too smart, ain't too dumb,
Outta the rain, here I come.

It's a habit, a hobby, how I like to pass the time. It's my house, so can't nobody tell me I'm disturbing the peace. You got opinions, best keep them to yourself.

When I grow parched and leave off for another pull, here come all these noises, rustling scratching thudding stomping. You got your gravely murmurs and your high-pitched squeals, your hollow clangs and your metallic clanks. Goddamn mice are at it again, I say, but that's a falsehood I'm telling myself, don't ask me why. Maybe I can't tolerate the idea of rats birds alley cats raccoons taking up residence without so much as a by your leave. Trespassers squatters interlopers leaving their mess all over my well-organized and semi-sanitary luxury attic space.

Like I say, got a man in my attic.

I sing me another tune, then smack bang throttle my guitar for a spell. Got two strings to pluck. The rest have gone missing, raccoons run off with them, perhaps, they got a nasty habit of picking locks and taking what ain't rightfully theirs. Not ever so different from the man in my attic, when you get down to it. Taking shelter power water just like filching a greasy twenty from the pocket of my dungarees while I'm sawing logs in front of the unlit stove, hugging the empty bottle to my chest.

I make my peace with the man in my attic for the time being. He's got his space up high, I got my space down low, and never the twain shall meet. Tolerate me all kinda hullaballoo clonking clumping thunking thumping. Shrieks and screams and blood-curdling giggles. Pipe down, I say. Button your lip, I say. Shut your pie-hole before I shut it for you, I say, though way back in the back of my throat and deep down under my breath. All that racket keeps me up during the day when I'd rather be resting my eyes. It interrupts my various evening pursuits and sundry nighttime endeavors, including newel-post whittling, beard scratching, elixir-bottle emptying.

But I put up with, tolerate, suffer all that noise. On not-so-rare occasion, I even welcome the clamor. You live alone, you like a diversion now and again. The man who lives in my attic has got him lots of buddies coming over once twice thrice a week. Got a little live-in hussy, too. So I don't mind some warm convivial noise leaking down through the rafters every now and again. Feels like festive company. Only it's too often too frenzied too loud. Imagine the undue stress and tension casting a pall over my cogitating time.

All that's bad enough already. But when the man in my attic starts in with the stink, enough's enough. I got fumes drifting down through the ceiling night and day. Green stink and gray stink red stink and brown stink, all rank as the day is long. Rotten cabbage and chewed-up garlic and vinegar mouthwash. Moldy cheese feet and stale coffee breath and fried-onion perfume. I have to keep a Kool burning so I don't get woozy green bilious from the constant flow of airborne funk.

I let it go for a week, maybe more. Cut a guy some slack, why don't you? That's the type of landlord I am. But it ain't long before I can't take no more. It's none of my doing. I come home from Our Lady of Grace and burn my last Kool, then tear up the empty carton to feed the fire. Now I'm fresh outta incense, so I know I gotta go up there and give it to him straight. The man in my attic. He's just your average freeloading squatter who don't pay enough attention to the consequences of his actions, namely, stinking up the breathable airspace.

It's spitting outside as I climb the outside stairs. Slate gray skies and a cold north wind. In the street, tires hiss along wet asphalt. I shiver quiver wipe my face with my old handkerchief, then set knuckles to glass. Don't rightly recall this fancy door from the remodel.

Scampering and slip-sliding on polished hardwood floors, then the hussy appears. Blonde braids and squishy lips and a set of titties to keep you safe in the deep dark night. But she don't come to the door like a polite kind respectful hussy. She just stands there, saucer-eyed jaw-dropped her porcelain face going all rosy.

Roger? she hollers, scuttling outta view. Roger!

I rap on the glass again. It's wet and cold and past time for a taste of tincture. I don't aim to get my dander up, but such appears to be the direction we're headed.

Now the man in my attic makes himself known. He's a good-looking sonuvabitch, too. Tall with thick, dark hair and goddamn teeth straighter than railroad ties. So white and bright, they make my eyes ache. Carries scotch in a cut-glass glass. Looks down on me from the attic door like I'm some kinda pestilence, but that ain't the way it's gonna be.

Now Mr. Sir, says I, you will kindly pay the rent.

So that's what you came for? he says.

I catch a glimpse of his hussy peering around the corner. Roger? she says. It's okay, babe.

In full, if you please, I say.

The man in my attic forces an equine laugh, setting his highball on the sideboard on a coaster. He digs his bifold outta his back pocket, pinching some greenbacks into a grubby fan. How much do you need? he asks.

That burns me up. He knows exactly how much. He's just sticking it to me. I! His landlord! He! My tenant! Who has taken up residence without the proper protocols and paperwork. Who keeps a roof over his head only by my good graces. He's showboating for his hussy, who's creeping closer to the attic door. The man she calls Roger stands there, gazing at me over his patrician nose, running a hand absently along his chiseled, clean-shaven jaw. Sticking it to me. It chaps my hide six ways to Sunday.

Roger? says the hussy, hiding behind the man's broad back.

He slips a muscled arm around her shoulders and hugs her to him. Nothing to worry about, babe, he says. Our landlord here—I'm sorry, I didn't catch your name?

Jimmy, says I.

Our landlord Jimmy—

James, Jim, Jimmyboy. Pick your poison.

The man in my attic gets the blank face. He deserves every bit of it, gazing down at me so high-and-mighty. Don't he realize who's in charge here? He could be out on his keister in nothing flat, alls I gotta do is snap my fingers and say the word. Only I ain't like that, I ain't like him, I give a feller the benefit of the doubt. We all got our ups and downs. We all got our days, good and bad.

James just came to collect the rent, sweetie.

You got that right! says I.

The hussy throws me a dirty look.

And I'm sure he's a very busy man, so if he'll just remind me what we agreed on, I'll take care of it, and he can be on his way.

Funny kinda way of talking, you ask me.

The man Roger waits. Cars slosh up and down the wet streets. The rain continues to rain. I hawk spit wipe my face with my handkerchief, then say:

All of it.

You mean—?

Everything.

His face tightens.

Ain't my duty to explain, but he don't seem to grasp the niceties, so I lay out the fine print. You got your first month's and your last month's, says I. You got your late rent and your late fees. Plus, the security. You ain't never paid the security on my newly renovated luxury attic apartment. Gotta cover my backside in case you and your hussy go and trash the place.

He can't talk about me like that, Roger!

The man in my attic wisely ignores the hussy. Good point, he says, digging out the thick stack of bills and passing them to me. Sorry for the misunderstanding. Won't happen again.

Good to know, says I, folding the wad into my greasy pocket. Better not. Plus, keep the noise down! Keep the stink down! No clogging during quiet hours!

The hussy stares daggers, but that's what hussies do. Plus, she ain't got no say. This business is between me and the man in my attic.

Downstairs, I light the stove and uncork a fresh bottle of elixir.

Next day, I come home from Our Lady of Grace to a real head-scratcher. My key don't seem to work. Slides in just right like always but won't turn, no matter how much I coax, persuade, jiggle. That's bad enough but ain't the end of nothing. Some joker's bolted on a big fat latch and secured it with one of them king-size Master Locks. As if this ain't my very own house home humble abode.

Get these spells now and again, so I double-check the location in case I'm on the wrong block, but all my ducks are in a row. Gray pickup across the street, fat ugly tomcat next door. I blink and wipe the wet from my face with my old handkerchief, then blink again. Blue Victorian with the gray trim. Used to be a gray Victorian with blue trim till I had her repainted, which is more confusion by half than anybody deserves.

Make me a note to self, then try the deadbolt again.

The key still don't work. Master Lock's still there and don't budge, not even when I diddle it with my lock blade. Need a big ugly crowbar for some leverage, but that ain't something I carry on my person regular. So there ain't nothing for it.

I unlock a window with a hunk of busted brick.

After that, I don't go out for a day or two or few, owing to the ingress-egress difficulty. They miss me at Our Lady of Grace, but I gotta look out for me and mine. Whole time, I'm working on that new deadbolt. Where'd it come from? Why's it here? Takes a few specialized tools that I ain't got, but I get her done anyhow. You gotta have focus, determination, perseverance. Take pride in a job well done. So I dismantle and remove that thing, then pitch it into the junk heap in the corner. Flaming flicker from the wood burning stove dances and jumps against that brass, bent and burnished.

When I finally lay hold of an old Phillips head, I let them latch screws have it, one after the other, till the whole thing tumbles into a metallic heap on the damp mossy concrete. You can't keep a good man down, no siree! Then I shove the door open, gather the lock and latch, fling it onto the junk heap with a metallic clang.

Now I'm off to the neighborhood Freddy's and back, brand-new deadbolt in a sack. I get that beauty into the door in nothing flat. In this game, you gotta be good with your hands, always something to fix install repair install fix. My shiny key shimmers in the firelight. I slam the door, throw the lock, grin till it hurts. Then I measure a scrap of cardboard from the junk heap, cut it to size with my lock blade, duck tape it over the broken window.

The man in my attic and his hussy host one shindig after the next, though the lease they never got around to signing mandates an absence of blustering blathering cackling top-of-the-lungs howling. They drown out my expert guitar picking. Can't hardly even hear my own quavering warbling phlegm-rich voice for all the racket.

Fat cat foreclosed and took my home.
What, oh what, will I become?

Happens one twice thrice then out comes the broom. Age-old time-honored solution to unruly tenant hullabaloo. I can't have what I'm having, so I let the man in my attic have it. His hussy, too. While it ain't all fun and games, it's what has to be done, such is the life of the homeowner lessor slumlord. They start banging, I bang back in a quieter, gentler, more mime-like fashion. Keep it down! I say. Quiet hours! I say. Don't make me call the cops! I say without raising my voice above a muted whisper. Then I uncap a fresh bottle of elixir. Takes all kinds, but a feller can only put up with so much. We all got our limits.

Ain't long thereafter, I come home from Our Lady of Grace to find an old coat on my doorstep. No note no tag no nothing. Thing reeks of veal marsala and swallows me whole, but it's fine wool with a big collar and lots of buttons. I take a quick glance around, right left over my shoulder, then I'm through the door. Finders, keepers. I throw the deadbolt light the fire pull my new coat tight around me like a blanket.

Next morning, there's more junk on my stoop. A sleeping bag and blanket, right outta nowhere. Figure somebody's using my front porch for a bedroom, though the sleeping bag's rolled up tight, and the blanket's folded and placed on top. Still, I know which way the wind blows even when there ain't no wind, so I don't touch nothing. Hobo Joe's off panhandling nearby, he'll be back when it suits him, I ain't fixing to come between him and his bedroll. Shiv to the eye, easy as pie.

When I come back from the neighborhood Freddy's with a tarp to cover the window-shaped hole, that bedroll's still sitting there, like its point is to ugly up the place. Been driving down property values all morning. So I gather it up and bring it indoors. Blanket smells like Tide mothballs must. Sleeping bag stinks of must mothballs campfire smoke. I huddle around the wood stove, sipping elixir and waiting for that dirty filthy no-good bum to come banging on my door, blaming me for thievery treachery and worse, but he's long gone, sleeping in hobo village under the 405, drunk on sweet wine in Chinatown, dead in a gutter on Burnside. Don't never put nothing past the undesirable element.

I rouse from a tonic stupor swaddled in my new bedroll, and outside my door I find more trash. This time a big-ole, greasy-ole paper bag. Inside, a compostable container full of half-eaten food. Spring rolls, drunken noodle, steamed rice, all cold congealed mixed up together. A big fat cold cowpie of Oriental muck. That's something new. Dumb yuppie's leftovers went missing and landed on my front porch. But I can't exactly leave them out there, attracting rats cockroaches vermin hobos and driving down the property values.

Same thing every day for a week. I stumble to my doorstep to find bags boxes to-go containers of every shape and size filled with half-eaten food. Half a cheeseburger and soggy French fries. A T-bone that ain't nothing but fat and gristle. Greasy egg rolls and fried rice without no chopsticks nor fortune cookie. One morning, I even discover a bag containing a box containing the biggest biscuit I ever set my peepers on. Weighs a ton. Search under behind around, rifle through the box and turn the bag inside out, but still I'm left wondering: Ain't you got no butter for this biscuit?

It's all like partial manna from halfway heaven—if, that is, you're a tramp a vagrant a hobo a bum. Only there ain't no down-and-outers around these parts, excepting the man in my attic. We got us a good neighborhood, out with the old, in with the new. Everybody bright shiny newly scrubbed garbed in the latest and greatest with a fresh haircut and straight from the dentist. Everything's going fancy dignified high-dollar uptown. We're ritzy and upscale, no two ways about it. Nothing to see, folks. Keep moving.

Then one morning, nothing. Zilcho. Where's the coagulated chicken chow mein? Where's the smear of spaghetti alla carbonara? Maybe some bum's filching the food-trash? I don't know whether to laugh or cry, but at least I don't have to fend off the alley cats cockroaches rats raccoons no more. We can't have vermin, including vagrants hobos derelicts bums roaming around, scarfing partially eaten leftovers. It ain't hygienic nor hypoallergenic, spreads diseases such as syphilis and the plague. Bad to get them critters hooked on handouts, too. Soon as that happens, you can say sayonara to your equity and your resale value. So when the restaurant slop dries up, I say good riddance to bad rubbish.

Only next thing I know, here comes a rap rap rapping on my chamber door. I'm lounging on my bedroll. A fire crackles in the stove. Empty bottles litter the floor, and I knock them down like bowling pins as I stagger across the room. Pull it open a crack, catch me a glimpse of the man Roger's hussy flitting away up the outside stairs to the attic entrance. She's got a long pair of legs that won't quit, plus a tasty rump, round firm squeezable. Watch her till she disappears into my attic so I almost set my boot smack-dab in the middle of a fresh hot homemade pie. Blueberry! Right out the oven! I pick that beauty up and give it a sniff. It ain't sloppy seconds from some sweet tooth date to Papa Hadyn, not on your life. This here's bona fide the real deal the genuine article, a gift a present a peace offering. Scrum-diddly!

That pie is sweet gooey sticky sweet. No question the hussy made it with real blueberries that grow out in nature, not them fake ones you find on the shelf in a can at the neighborhood Freddy's. Even the crust tastes like it's made from scratch. I eat and eat till I can't eat no more because there ain't no more pie left, then I wash her down with a fresh bottle of elixir, huddling round the fire in my new stinky wool coat. I'm toasty warm and sticky-fingered, my gut aching, a contented smile stretching my cheeks. I listen to the crackle of the burning wood, dozing and dreaming of Szechuan chicken California rolls combination burritos Korean barbecue. Hog heaven!

As for the doorstep trash-dumping? Mystery solved.

Later, much later, when I wake up, the gut ache's completely gone, but I still got the ghost of blueberry sweetness lingering under my sandpaper tongue. That don't change nothing bout what I gotta do. You're a landlord, you got responsibilities. Goes with the territory. First and foremost is protecting your property value, since without value, your property's worthless. But a close second is keeping your tenants in line. They don't toe the line, they get outta line, you gotta put them back on the straight and narrow. That's a chore, no question. But you let it go for long, they'll try to get away with murder. So I grab the empty pie plate, hug that stinky wool around me, and slip out the door. My breath plumes in the wet cold as I slink up the outside steps to the attic door. You can't underestimate the power of surprise. That's the way you catch them tenants red-handed, mangy mutts water bongs friends colleagues associates sleeping on the couch on the floor in the bathtub. I try my key, but the man in my attic has changed the locks, yet another strike against him and his hussy. That's when I give it the business end of my lock blade. A mean ole heavy ole crowbar would be better, but I make do.

Inside, all's quiet. Smell of orange blossoms and cinnamon drifts on the warm air. I linger next to the radiator for a spell, warming my fingers toes derriere. From what I can tell, the man in my attic has really spruced the place up. Sectional sofa Persian rugs wall pictures the works. Not bad for a lousy dirty filthy no-good squatter. Before all's said and done, he'll sign the lease and pay up on time every month, or I'll boot his sorry ass to the curb. His hussy's, too—though I'd much rather squeeze on it for a spell.

When feeling tingles back into my extremities and I start gagging on the potpourri, I set the pie plate on a counter and wade through the dim murk toward the bedroom. Smack into end tables, thump into walls, knock a pot bowl vase to the parquet floor where it shatters to smithereens. What happened to the plush wall-to-wall? Who's to blame for this crazy floor plan? The man Roger is really taking liberties, exploiting my patience benevolence goodwill. Probably his hussy's notion. They're both in way over their heads.

I trip and stagger through my attic, groping at walls, pawing door facings. Time marches on, and my vision ain't what it used to be. Plus, the man Roger and his hussy keep this place dark as death. Only light streams in in slivers beneath the window slats. I could throw all the switches, but the wily sonuvabitch probably tied his electrical in with mine, so guess who'd be footing the bill?

The bedroom's right where empty space used to be. I stand over the bed, sipping from my bottle of elixir, locking and unlocking my lock blade. The man Roger might be a good-looking sonuvabitch, but he snores like a buzzsaw. It's a wonder the hussy can stand it. I take me another pull of elixir, then set myself to singing.

Home & hearth, hearth & home,
Wherever I be, wherever I roam.

That rouses the hussy outta her REM. She peels back her mask, all squinty-eyed and squishy-lipped, fussing with the covers. Got them a fine blanky, soft fuzzy warm velour and big as a football field. Notch or two up from my mothball-stinking hand-me-down bedroll. My lock blade glints in the dim yellow streetlight leaking in around the window slats. I watch the hussy go tense all except for them titties when she notices me. Porcelain face looks like it might crack any minute now.

Roger! she says, whispering like I can't hear every word. He don't move, just keeps on with the racket. She punches him in the shoulder. Roger!

The man in my attic snorts, then hollers, Tag Heuer! Now he leans up on one elbow, smacking and rubbing his eyes. What is it, babe?

He's here, says the hussy.

He smacks again. What?

The man, she says between her teeth.

What man, babe?

I think he's got a knife.

When I've had enough, I say, Keep on talking like I can't hear you.

The fridge hums. The clock ticks. A lone car hisses along the wet asphalt.

My wallet's on the nightstand, says the man Roger.

That's mighty generous, I say, but I only want what I got coming to me. I lean over to the end table, set down my empty bottle, pocket my lock blade. Now I stretch open that bifold and liberate this month's rent. Maybe I'm grinning chuckling licking my chops because the man in my attic sits up and clicks on a lamp.

Now that's the end of it, says the man Roger. No more.

Why he takes that tone is beyond me. There's only one man in charge in the driver's seat running the show, and that man's me.

Not if you plan to continue occupying my attic, it ain't.

Your what? says the hussy.

You gotta pay on time every month and follow the rules and regulations to a T. That's the way this whole thing works. Mind your P's and Q's. It's all spelled out in the lease if you woulda took the time to read it.

I reach for the bottle of elixir till I remember it's already dry. The man Roger's face is a sour pucker. His hussy clings to his side like they're standing on the edge of a cliff. Come to think of it, they just might be.

Let me sum up, I explain. No trash on the stoop. No ruckus or stink-making. Keep them pies coming.

Their faces look pale tired droopy.

Easy-peasy, says I. You take care of your business, I'll take care of mine, everything'll be peaches and cream. I reach out and pinch that velour, run it between my fingers. That sure is a nice blanky you got there, by the by.

You can have it if you like, says the hussy. Just say the word.

Don't think I miss the funny look the man Roger tosses her.

The hussy slides outta bed, got nothing on but a big ole t-shirt and itty-bitty shorts, I can't take my eyes off them thighs. She yanks the blanky off the bed, then throws it over my shoulders. I pull it snug, though there's too much of it. Thing's thick soft warm and smells like Tide.

Thank you kindly, I say.

The man in my attic sneers. You got more than you came for, he says. Don't make me call the police.

Roger!

Don't nobody talk to me like that, I say.

You're in my house, so I'll—

Whose house? I say.

Roger! the hussy says again.

You've worn out your welcome, Jamesy Boy or whatever your name is.

Landlord suits me fine.

Time to go, Jimbo.

I stuff the cash in my front pocket, then pull my lock blade back out, fold it open, run my thumb along the blade. I keep her nice and sharp. The hussy eases back to the far side of the bed. I hawk and spit on the polished hardwoods. Then I say, Up.

The front door's that—

Don't make me ask twice, says I. We're burning daylight.

The man in my attic gets himself upright. He's a full head taller than me with better reach, but who's got the lock blade? His hussy cowers behind him. Squishy lips shiny thighs titties thick soft warm, but ain't none of that in the lease. I make a mental note for future reference. You gotta revise the paperwork from time to time.

Keys, I say.

What do you—?

Don't want no more of your lip. Now gimme your keys, both of you.

Maybe I'm no great shakes at the lessor-lessee relationship, but soon I got a fistful of jangle. Now I march the man in my attic and his hussy to the door. Consider yourselves hereby forthwith and posthaste evicted, as per the lease agreement you never read signed returned. Then by the glinting point of my lock blade, I force them out the door, the man Roger blustering empty protests, his hussy weeping into his chiseled chest. It's much ado about nothing, since Our Lady of Grace ain't but a couple-three blocks away, where they got a bed and hot meal waiting for them.

I throw the deadbolt wrench the curtains clamp the window slats, then rummage around the kitchen for a cool bottle of elixir. Alls I find is a lousy half-bottle of sweet wine in the fridge. Figures, don't it?

Soon I settle into bed, silk sheets and feather pillows, still wrapped in all that warm clean fuzzy velour. I sip and drowse, sip and drowse, sip and drowse in my thick warm blanky in my soft warm bed in my safe warm luxury attic apartment. Ain't never felt so calm relaxed peaceful at ease in all my days, not that I rightly recall. What they call bliss. I listen to the patter of rain on the roof. I listen to the slosh of tires on wet asphalt. I listen to the pale scream of sirens howling in the wet dark morning.

poem

Holiday Cheer
xavier stone

"The British survived The Somme,
we can survive this,"
I yell to the wall.

Blood mixes with water; violently swirling, bubbling,
foaming in the pan I hold, spray clean of debris,
and feed to the growling, boiling, hissing machine
permanently guarding my left flank
from memories of dryness.

I feel the floor shift slightly
when the line cooks echo,
 "86 Nachos!"
Followed too soon by, "86 Wings!"

Dinner rush is still at least two hours away.

Water beads against my plastic apron
after ricocheting off a ladle.

Dishwashing involves a surprising
amount of mathematics. But I cannot calculate
how I will subtract the scent of pico de gallo
from my shirt, my boots, my skin.

I wonder if the customers
think of the irony that for them
to be eating tomato, onion, and cilantro
on December 25th means that the restaurant staff must work.

There is no calm before the storm. Everything crashes in too suddenly.

"86 Burgers!"
"86 Mashed!"
"86 my will to live!"
"86 Ice Cream!"
"86 Joy!"
"86 Beans!"
"86 Happiness!"

I wrestle a rack of silverware onto a countertop.

There's a shift.

Almost a catch.

Silverware shatters the expected drone of the kitchen.

I turn to grab towels to use as gloves,
planning to scoop up the cutlery
like snow in open palms.

"STOP! Where's the blood coming from?" the other dishwasher bellows.

Beneath the fluorescent lights, the crimson of myself staining
knife handles, contaminating fork tines, all reflect in a way
that reminds me of Christmas lights.

Bona Fide Hustlin'

brendan praniewicz

BONA FIDE HUSTLIN'

May 2008, we gathered under a punch-blue sky as the department chair and dean read our names over a raspy microphone. My classmates, the greatest minds of my generation, looked eager and excited, strolling across that big stage, enamored by the moment, and waving at sobbing parents.

Far behind my colleagues, I tapped my foot to Pomp and Circumstance. Warm shots of whiskey trickled through my veins. What the hell had I accomplished?

I had no money, no job, no time to mess around. Between thirty grand in school loans, maxed out credit cards, and a wedding on the horizon, I felt submerged in "near collection agency" debt. What had I done with the past three years of my life? My thesis, although officially signed off, only amounted to a half written, soppy memoir. My residence was a bathroom-sized trailer, my diet consisted of canned anything, and instead of preparing for the real world, I focused on writing fiction that never sold.

Through it all, I obtained my goal—a Master of Fine Arts degree in Creative Writing from San Diego State.

Deep down I felt aimless, clueless, spun out in career vertigo—certified screwed.

What does one do with a Creative Writing degree? I avoided this question throughout college. I figured writers were employable because they had to figure out everything: every known species of birds, the history of the combustion engine, the laws of thermodynamics, the evolving cultural constructions of vampires and werewolves—the list was infinite. Most writers I knew didn't need money—they thrived off glimmering optimism.

In 2008, America suffered a bad case of arrogance and naïveté, and I wasn't immune. I saw no reason to fixate on anything less than perfection and entitlement. I sent out my resume a month before graduation, cut my hair, bought deodorant, and shaved my Karl Marx beard. I began my occupational pursuit with my foot firmly planted on lofty expectations—no middle-management gigs and no living on commission. I wouldn't accept any time-consuming job that hindered my ability to write. As a young artist entering high society, the world owed me something. To this effect, I wasn't surprised when my first big interview came fast.

I received an offer to work as a personal trainer at an "experimental gym," but when I arrived for my interview, I was amazed to find no treadmills, no weights, no pink sit-up balls. What kind of gym was this? The room looked desolate with the exception of a few machines resembling foot scales with handlebars.

My interviewer, a plump Australian woman, boldly announced these contraptions were "Power Plates"—innovative workout machines designed to flatten flabby fannies by shaking the living daylights out of them.

"These buggers are used to improve circulation, posture, and NASA invented them," she spouted.

After revving up the machine, I stood on the platform. My toes vibrated as if placed in a Jacuzzi. I glanced at my pulsating sneakers and stumbled on a grand epiphany: this bugger did nothing for me. How could I honestly look this enthusiastic "trainer" in the eyes and explain I saw no future in Power Plates? No one would pay money for this. She looked so jubilant, standing on the contraption, vibrating profusely.

I gazed around the room and saw diplomas scattered across the wall: helicopter pilot degrees. No wonder she enjoyed vibrating. Was she even qualified to run a gym? Something didn't seem right.

When the interview ended, I rejected her proposal, although she offered eighteen dollars an hour under the table. The bottom: if I didn't buy the idea behind something, then I refused to sell it to others.

Looking back, I should've accepted the job.

After that first interview, nobody called. I frantically searched for work, certain my education would prevail. I grew desperate and backed out of my "no management/no commission" promise. If I had to, I'd sell my soul for minimum wage.

"Why are you applying for a sales position when you have a degree in creative writing?" A presumptuous woman for Xerox once asked me over the phone.

"Apparently, I sold you on my resume or else you wouldn't be calling me." I felt proud of this response but dismayed when the woman hung up on me.

During these discouraging moments, I held steady to a pep rally speech my high school principal once presented. "Look here kids, someone with a high school education averages a thousand more a month than a dropout." Pointing to a pay chart, he continued, "And, by golly look here, a person with a BA makes a thousand more monthly than someone with a GED." This monetary encouragement continued through MA's, MBA's, and PhD's all amounting to that additional cool grand. My principal always finished speeches with the random assertion: "Listen boys and girls, education offers you two tools—a moral compass and a career compass."

Being a writer, I didn't have morals, but the career compass intrigued me. Not to mention, his "House that Jack Built" pyramid instilled in me that the path to education lead to vast opulence and literary fame.

By July, I sent my resume to more than a hundred companies and colleges, but nothing promising returned. A high-end San Diego career agency promised to find me a lucrative career if I paid them seven grand, and a low-end temp agency found me a job drawing caricatures at SeaWorld.

Short on food and rent, I searched everywhere for a decent job. Budget cuts and layoffs resulted in an already flooded market. I was overqualified for most positions, and my resume, a stockpile of dead-end jobs, lead nowhere. I desperately searched for work in an economy gone sour, falling face-first into an unforeseen recession.

THERE IS NO I IN STARBUCKS

"The world is going to hell, dude," Johnny C enjoyed prophesizing at 4AM as we stood outside Starbucks, waiting for our manager.

Johnny C, my gay coworker, stood 5'2, with daunting blue eyes, and cocaine-like energy. He had silver customer service awards, shaped like coffee mugs, pinned to his apron, and he loved to flaunt them.

"Do you see what's going on in this city?" Johnny C continued. "The middle class is shrinking. Do you know what happens when there's no middle class? Revolution."

"Yeah, but no matter what happens, Johnny C, people will always need coffee," I answered. "Or else you and me wouldn't be standing out here at four God damn o'clock in the morning."

"You got that right, dude."

"Look on the bright side. We're going to caffeinate World War III."

Johnny C had natural energy. He zoomed around the store without the aid of illegal drugs or the superpowers of caffeine. Johnny C arrived in neat dress shirts and khakis devoid of coffee stains. He ironed his clothes before coming to work. Who the hell irons their Starbuck's uniform at 2:30 in the morning? Johnny C was an anomaly and management loved him.

On the other hand, management despised me. Always on the verge of getting written up, I spent my time on bar, slipping shots of espresso in between drinks for customers. I arrived to work in coffee stained-cargo shorts and a wrinkled shirt, reeking of sour milk. I needed every ounce of energy to arrive downtown before dawn. Every morning I drove to work, blasting music, asking myself, "What the hell am I doing with my life?" I never imagined my career compass would steer me back to God-awful Starbucks.

After graduating college, I promised that no matter how bad life became, I'd never be a barista again. I worked at Starbucks in a mall one summer and still had flashbacks of greedy eight-year olds, rallying around the register for caramel frapps. Alanis Morrissette became the background music to my nightmares.

I returned to caffeine incorporated at the end of my rope, desperately needing money, and that half-naked, controversial mermaid sweetly chanted my name.

Working at a downtown Starbucks during the morning rush was like sailing a sinking ship. From 7:00 to 10 AM came the hellbound express—a line of angry customers frothed from the register to the sidewalk. Our clientele consisted of angry attorneys quick to speak their misanthropic minds. I spent the majority of my shift sprinting to garbage cans, wiping up turd-colored mocha, and shelling out Americanos in nanoseconds.

While juggling these labors, I faced the carb-burning task of feeding the parking meter. Every two hours I charged out of the door jangling a pocketful of quarters. One morning my truck got towed, and this defeat nearly devoured my whole paycheck—three hundred dollars.

On top of that, my assistant manager possessed all of the natural talents of running a torture chamber. Behind her ever-present poker face, I believed she secretly fantasized about killing me. Johnny C and I called her CBT (Charlie Brown's Teacher). She grumbled her demands, and we had no idea what she desired. CBT barked orders over the machine gun barrage of the coffee grinder, self-righteous customers screaming over foamless lattes, and the ninja steam shooting espresso machine. I responded, while ducking behind milk carafes and half-empty sugar jars, shouting: "What? What? Okay!"

One memorable morning, a crotchety old man stumbled into the store. He wore a WWII Veteran hat, and he stood before the register picking his teeth with his pinky and grunted, "Give me a big ass cup of Joe."

While I punched in his order, I noticed the man glaring at Johnny C, who waltzed with a mop to Dido's song lyrics, "I will go down with this ship."

"What's up with this clown?" the customer asked with John Wayne-like swagger.

"I don't know." I shrugged and handed the vet his change. "He just likes to dance."

The old vet scratched his head and stormed toward Johnny C. What followed a long homophobic tirade degrading my coworker in the crudest terms. I stood, dumbfounded, behind the register over hearing bits of dogmatic slurs. Johnny C sat there, rather composed, no rebuttal.

The irony of this situation—the week before we'd completed a computer module on sexual harassment, but the module only covered employer/employee harassment. What about customer sexual harassment? While the vet verbally harassed Johnny C, no one knew what to do. I looked for CBT to intervene, but she covered her mouth, trying not to laugh.

After the veteran strutted out of the store, I huddled next to Johnny C. His eyes drifted to his green apron. He straightened his customer service awards. "Don't console me, dude," he whispered. "I've put up with homophobes like that my whole life."

I felt terrible. After watching my assistant manager laugh while my coworker was lambasted, I now loathed CBT.

A week later I quit.

On my last day at Starbucks, any customer who gave me a hard time received decaf. That six shot "attorney" Americano was nobody's savior that morning. During my final hours, I pictured San Diego's finest passing out behind their gargantuan desks—victims of a local barista let down.

After turning in my uniform, I stepped outside on a crisp Saturday with a pocketful of change. Four miserable months had passed since I graduated, and I finally moved on to something bigger and better. Downtown San Diego seemed so quiet; a city hung over from the night before. While the masses slept, the world seemed filled with limitless possibility.

ADVENTURES IN FREEDOM FIGHTING

I'd landed a new job that paid three more dollars an hour. I was now a "Lobby Ambassador," also known as "Freedom Fighter," also known as "Security Guard." I worked at a high-rise in downtown San Diego, wore a suit and tie to work, and spent the majority of my shift hunting Osama bin Laden in the parking garage. Thanks to me, our building remained crime-free, with the exception of one incident where a terrorist made off with a handful of Christmas cookies.

Security was laid back. I loved working nights and weekends, which gave me more time to read and write. My career compass landed me the most lucrative writing job I'd had.

As a writer, "observe and report" came natural for me, and I had front row seats to the class divide. The high-rise consisted of law firms and high-end investment companies—a place where worlds often collided. Every morning I observed high profile people glide into the lobby, wearing thousand-dollar suits, while outside the window, homeless people scuffled down the sidewalk, looking for change and pushing shopping carts. My job entailed making sure that those worlds remained far apart.

When I started, I thought I had an important role in protecting the wealthy from impoverished miscreants, but in the grand scheme of things, security guards received no respect on either end. Every week either a lawyer or transient cursed me with threats or wanted to fight me.

One overcast Saturday I approached a gang of skaters. As soon as I pulled out my walkie-talkie, the younger kids darted in different directions, but a big tubby kid wearing a Charger jersey stood defiantly with one foot on his board.

"There's no skateboarding here." I pointed to a red and white sign that practically screamed: "No posers on property."

The kid retorted in a scratchy voice, "Oh yeah, I bet you can't even read that sign. You're just a dumbass security guard."

Ten years of college never prepared me for this. Five months prior I worked as a grad student teaching students a few years older than this kid reading and comprehension at San Diego State. Now I had this child not only questioning my literacy but looking down on me for being a security guard?

The kid skated circles around me with taunts and insults until he finally ended with, "I bet I have a higher GPA than you."

Anger swelled deep within my chest as I wanted to defend myself. Instead, I mumbled, "There's no way you have a higher GPA than me." I felt degraded as the child chuckled and hopped on the trolley.

Disenchanting moments happened nearly every day. I tried not to take incidents personally, but finding myself belittled on a daily basis, my self-esteem dwindled, and I despised what I'd become.

After my shift I often stopped at 7-11 to buy a six-pack of booze. I needed something to ease all of the turmoil and disappointment that brewed deep inside. I spent years working hard at school, hoping that it would pay dividends, but never imagined graduating and working security. During these months of despair, I had severe bouts of depression. Nearly every night I watched stand-up comedy under the stupor of a warm beer buzz. I looked to comedy to lift my spirits. Dane Cook and old clips of Eddie Murphy provided some comic relief. I often watched stand-up for hours straight without laughing. Sometimes I cried.

WHEN A HOUSE OF CARDS COLLAPSES

During the month of December, I started a new valet job at the Hyatt downtown.

One morning I drove to work, and my stomach hurt like hell. The night before I devoured 7-11 sushi and washed it down with Arrogant Bastard Ale. I passed my stomach pain off as indigestion and decided to power through work. When I arrived at the hotel, the pain grew unbearable, and I told my boss that running for cars was out of the question. I had a bad case of diarrhea, and customers already griped if I left sweat marks on their leather interior.

That evening I worked my slower-paced security job, but my stomach pain traversed from stabbing to psychotic gashing. Maybe I had food poisoning again? Extreme dehydration? I downed a bottle of Gatorade, hoping the pain would dissipate.

The next morning it hurt to walk, but with Christmas around the corner, I worked my security job because I needed money. I performed patrols, trembling in nauseating pain and went home shivering and sweating. With no desire to know what ailed me, I refused pain relievers and didn't take my temperature. I chose not to acknowledge the problem because I didn't have health insurance.

When I worked security Sunday night, I pretended nothing hurt. My hernia, ulcer, cancer was all a figment of my imagination. I moved sluggishly but smiled with foolish delusion. I tried to trick myself into believing that my stomach didn't hurt and told myself even cartwheels seemed possible.

The severity of the situation arose when I accidentally locked myself in the high-rise stairwell. The pain intensified as I trudged down 32 flights of stairs. At one point, I nearly passed out.

I arrived home that night, and my fiancé wrangled me to the floor. She wrenched a thermometer in my mouth. I stared in disbelief as my temperature reached 103 degrees.

By the time my fiancé drove me to the hospital, my fever hit 104.

I clutched my stomach, limped towards the ER receptionist, and groaned, "I can't afford this."

Sitting in a hospital bed waiting for the doctor, I discussed possible alternatives with my fiancé. "Take me to Tijuana. Let's go home and look up really high fever on Wikipedia. Assisted suicide?"

Two hours later an MRI revealed a ruptured appendix. I had no idea what this meant and pleaded with my fiancé to drag me to the car.

"You don't understand the urgency here," the doctor replied. "A ruptured appendix is fatal."

After this bold affirmation, everything became fuzzy. The word fatal rang through my mind as I signed dizzying amounts of paperwork. I remember squeezing my fiancé's hand before going to surgery. I vaguely recall an anesthesiologist explaining, "Welcome to your party. Let's start with a round of margaritas."

Thirty minutes later I woke up in the worst pain ever. My throat felt rubbed raw. It hurt to breathe. I wondered if my doctor had accidentally sewn his surgical tools into my intestines.

For two days I lingered in the hospital, high on painkillers, watching Frank TV and giggling at his Charles Barkley impressions. Laughing hurt more than anything, but I needed humor almost more than medicine.

When the hospital released me, I felt numb and dizzy. I looked disheveled with knotted hair and drool on my chin. During my two-day stay, I told my nurse not to bathe me to cut the cost.

After my release, I hobbled to the financial aid sector of the hospital and glared at the receptionist. "I can't afford this," I shouted, pointing at my side.

My medical bills exceeded thirty thousand dollars. My total debt, school loans and all, exceeded sixty grand, and my six-month paper trail started here.

Tax returns, hospital bills, check statements, grocery and gas receipts—mounds of expectations exceeding thirty to sixty pages of redundant documentation. Every time I received a new application, an ominous voice declared, "You have ten days to complete and return this. Or else!" I felt trapped inside a Kafka novel where my proof of innocence was downplayed, and the in-your-face-bureaucracy never relented. Getting out of hospital bills seemed equivalent to the time and effort of working a full-time job.

Two weeks later, I quit valet because my boss grew tired of watching me limp for cars, and other kids were smoking me for tips. Quitting worked to my advantage because the less I worked, the better I looked on paper.

I had to prove that I made less than twenty grand a year in order to show that I could not pay the hospital $30,000. I was "lucky" that during my graduate year of university teaching, I only made six-hundred dollars a month in income, so I had, on record, proof that I was well below the poverty line. Agencies monitored my accounts. I couldn't pick up work or make money, because I had to prove that I didn't have any monetary sources to pay my bill. I spent vigorous hours laundering the little money I earned like a criminal.

County Medical Services rejected me twice for excessive income. My applications remained unprocessed for four months. Collection agencies began harassing me.

"Look here, we can work this bill out, so you'll have it paid off in no time. Give us thirteen thousand dollars down, and we'll set you at six-hundred-dollar monthly payments." The first time I heard this I laughed. Never in my life had I compiled a lump sum of thirteen grand.

When collections inquired about personal possessions, I stopped laughing. They encouraged me to declare bankruptcy. But that would ruin me financially for seven years? I was already 31 years old.

Throughout this whole fiasco, I stuck to my plea, "I can't afford this."

In the end my adamant response paid dividends.

The first week of June was one of the luckiest weeks of my life. I opened my mailbox and found a letter: my hospital bills were covered. I owed nothing. I expected that I'd at least have to pay something, but the hospital wrote my bill off. I've never felt that free in my entire life. Fighting this bill consumed six months of my life.

LOOK ALIVE OUT THERE

After taking care of my medical bills, I focused on setting up a teaching position. I missed the academic atmosphere, standing before a classroom, and lecturing on my favorite subject: writing. My real-world experience taught me that education was a wonderful profession, and even if I didn't make a lot of money, teaching brought fulfillment.

In 2008 and 2009 California made drastic cuts in education, and job prospects looked dismal. I now had a whole new battle on my hands.

Getting a teaching job required research, creativity, and playing different angles. Much of this depended on the "who you know" factor. I had a few connections, but this didn't help. Nobody was hiring. All summer I pestered department chairs, showed up at office hours, and sent out weekly emails. One time I emailed a department chair after receiving a rejection letter: "I am a damn good teacher, and I'll work ten times harder than anyone you interview."

Perhaps persistence won out in the end. I had nothing to lose, everything to gain, and after returning from the dead, both physically and financially, I had nothing to fear. By fall 2009 I taught at two local community colleges despite budget cuts, fierce competition, and weekly rejection.

Ten years have passed since I graduated. Today, I'm teaching at numerous colleges. As a part-time adjunct, I've had several classes cut, and I've lost positions at other colleges because of budget cuts. At this point there is no guarantee that I have a future in teaching, and this brutal truth makes me strive harder to become a better teacher, writer, and academic.

I have no idea where my career compass is pointing me. Every day I feel like I'm playing chess with all of the pieces in the air, not sure how everything will fall into place.

Since graduating, I've watched the greatest minds of my generation bus tables at restaurants, shelve books at bookstores, and bag groceries. Most of my fellow colleagues are teaching five to six classes and moonlighting as Uber drivers. We are a new breed of Americans, averaging forty-seven-hour work weeks, trying to survive in a city where the average rent is two grand, and the average house is $580,000.

It's challenging to believe the economy is stronger when people's incomes rely on driving random strangers in cars or renting out their apartments on weekends to people they've never met before. Our wages haven't increased while every day gets more expensive. The only certainty I have about the future: there is no certainty.

My grandparents, survivors of the Great Depression, squeezed every dime they had and hid money deep inside their bedroom walls—post traumatic stress that they never recovered from.

I wonder what scars our generation will carry.

Concrete Man

jim cole

It can be done during sleep. It was. I. No, not I. Dr. Intesa Sicurezza and I, we pursued this research for many years, this dream. Together, we unraveled the question, bringing it to its natural end: this. Success, proof. And now soon—in a matter of hours—publication.

We did not quit. I don't declare this fact lightly. No, against early setbacks, and against the unending doubts about our hypothesis, and against questions as to our scientific rigor, and against the name calling, insinuations and demonizing, no, we did not quit. And, even against the nefarious slanders aimed at our facility—this, our home, our laboratory, which, I admit, began as nothing more than a vacant warehouse between a smoky takeout barbecue and a tire recycler—no, we did not quit. How, you ask. How could anyone conduct research so vital to humankind sandwiched between Napoleon's BBQ and a Ulysses Tire franchise? As the profound Dr. Intesa Sicurezza said, Judge me not by my neighbors, but by the virtue of my deeds! So fond of quoting the scripture, a religious woman Dr. Intesa Sicurezza was not—saintly, yes.

Our detractors in the scientific community found infinite time and marshalled maniacal energy to undermine our groundbreaking work. What, we wondered aloud, of their own tepid research projects? They must have pawned off their monitoring and measuring on mushy-minded college interns, so they themselves could pursue their shenanigans and spiteful games at our expense. They tried to confound us. Oh, how they tried. A barrage of dubious news reports, snooping inspectors, and adolescent missives by quasi-scientists to the quasi-editors of quote-unquote scientific journals served only to delay our progress and prolong the inevitable, and at times pushed our resolve to the brink. Yet, I never lost faith. In the face of adversity, I never so much as questioned my devotion to Dr. Intesa Sicurezza. No, I never once wavered, and if ever so slightly then rightly so during what I've labeled the Gulliver Incident.

Here tonight, alone in our facility, I count the hours and minutes until dawn and the publication of our findings for the world to read. No sunrise ever felt so rejuvenating, no night so endless. The anticipation, the anticipation. If I may borrow lightly from Joseph Conrad. As the minutes claw past, I hunt and peck my story on this keyboard, finalizing a devoted scientist's journal, a memoir, as impassioned as any lover's confession. I am practically one now with this dark building. This laboratory—my sanctuary, my cell, my life and more—is illuminated by two feeble lights. The red glow of the smoke detector winks ironically high over my head, and above the infamous backdoor the green sign taunts me with its constant and heartless command

"EXIT."

I was warned many times that the taste of success could be sweet and sour, full of both the joyous sense of vindication and the unbearable tonnage of not being. "Done" is a crushing word. The realization that there is nothing ahead. Like the end of a great novel. Now, nothing is possible. There is no subsequent step or procedure to advance our findings, no hypothesis left to test, no axiom to validate, and no reversing what we have done to me. Our contribution to humankind is final. Once the results are published—silencing at last our critics, the most vocal of which has been Dr. Hand Kierkenes (Lunatic! Lunatic! Lunatic! There I've gotten that off my chest.)—then our life's work will be done.

Dr. Hand Kierkenes is a man with large ears and a moon-shaped head. That recombinant pairing associated throughout history with two types: smart men and idiots. He sports a well-groomed beard and very small hands. In his presence, the courageous Dr. Intesa Sicurezza once huddled in a circle of her male peers at a cocktail party and called him "Gerbil Hands." I, being socially awkward and a borderline introvert, refrained from joining Dr. Sicurezza at such networking events, which she deemed sources of invaluable intelligence and professional gossip that might contribute to our project's success. When she returned from what she called these "forays into social science," she always shared her insights with me, including the effect her ingenious sense of humor had upon those in attendance. I trace Dr. Kierkenes' juvenile and misguided hostility to our project to the now famous Gerbil Hands remark.

This rodent of a researcher works next door in his own little laboratory. Dr. Kierkenes is a latecomer and unwelcome in our flourishing research park, having secured funds last year from a shadowy third party to acquire and renovate the former tire franchise. On nights like tonight, when I am here alone with the smells of cayenne pepper and cold pork fat in my nostrils and images in my brain of spiders working their way up the cold concrete walls and back home to eat their young, I hear startling bursts from Dr. Hand Kierkenes' steam vents. One can only guess what caustic and unintended byproducts of his baffled brainwork he flushes into the atmosphere shrouded in the afterburn of Napoleon's BBQ.

On my keypad, just above the DELETE button where the ON-OFF usually sits, Dr. Sicurezza installed a red HELP button and promised me that in an emergency someone will come if I hold down that button for three seconds. What could constitute an emergency now in my condition? The mere appearance some nights of Dr. Kierkenes has tempted me to smash that red salvation. This man with his Norwegian cologne and four-foot-long phrases that flow like corn oil out of his chapped lips smelling like cod. How, I ask, did the devil incarnate get his hands on a key to our private laboratory in the first place?

"Intesa's results are bogus, Jerome," Dr. Kierkenes whispered in my ear last Saturday night. "Bogus, bogus, bogus! And nothing you imagine will be published will convince the public, much less, the scientific establishment that sweet Miss Sicko-Rezza is a true scientist, because she is not! Not, not, not! Your colleague is a lunatic. Do you hear me, Jerome? Lunatic, lunatic, nutso! And, you've been had."

He held up a photograph, which could only be an expensive forgery. I will describe it here not to give it credence, but rather so that if it finds its way into a publication that circulates beyond the checkout counter of the White Stallion Liquor Store, the public will have this record that the photo is fake. Fake. Fake. Fake.

First and foremost, a fact: Dr. Intesa Sicurezza does not dine out. Who would know better than I, her long-term research partner and eternal confidant? The photo Gerbil Hands held out for me to study that night was a winter scene, and yet the woman pictured wears a short white skirt and high heels, impractical footwear in which I never saw the pragmatic Dr. Sicurezza, and certainly not after Labor Day. And her hair, rather than being appropriately pinned in a tight bun as was laboratory protocol, dangled long and curled like some sort of tropical vegetation. It was in a style that I believe is known in urban slang as "a perm." Shorthand, I presume, for permutation. Preposterous. The woman etched for all eternity in that daguerreotype was not my Dr. Intesa Sicurezza of Tuscany by way of Tucson. Mark my words.

Were we to overlook the blatant inconsistencies in this forgery and turn our attention instead to the more salacious elements of the photo, we would quickly deem the image laughable and the situation it depicts an impossible slander. Dr. Intesa Sicurezza never dated. She never spoke to me of another man, there is no record of another man, no recorded instance of the Doctor spending time with another man, or publicly expressing an interest in another man. Dr. Intesa Sicurezza had me. Me, Dr. Jerome Glomma, Dr. Intesa Sicurezza's lab mate. Period.

Knowing this, the fabrication Dr. Kierkenes showed me was nothing more than his typical lunacy. Dr. Sicurezza, or her likeness, I should say at this point, sits in a well-known French wine bar—do people honestly patronize such establishments?—and between the hem of her short ivory colored skirt and her matching stiletto heels stretches, for all to see, black nylon stockings that appear made of fish nets (proof, perhaps, the image was concocted by the cod-loving Dr. Kierkenes). Beneath the table, her finely sculpted, if not perfectly sculpted, legs are crossed and on her left knee rests the simian paw of Dr. Kierkenes' associate, Sammy Verdeaux.

Now, let me declare for all perpetuity that up to that moment I felt no ill will toward my dear, albeit troubled, former college classmate Sam Verdeaux. Sam Verdeaux had dropped out of school and spent a decade traveling, only to reappear with a PhD from an Eastern Bloc university no one had heard of. He quickly became known in the scientific community as The Little Frenchman, or Le Petite Frenchie.

Oh, if only I could undo our final experiment and march out of this lab, I would have big words for this petite one, who was always up to no good.

He used to come around at the most inopportune moments, when I was tied down, for example, and Dr. Intesa Sicurezza was attempting one of her delicate and daring infusions. Her gaze through the shatter-proof glass of the test chamber would catch mine as the air began to turn gray with the swirling dust (in those earliest weeks, from simple and unrefined gypsum or alabaster). The fine powder tickled the hairs on my arms and private parts and began to penetrate my protective mask, causing my eyes to tear up, which in turn fogged the glass on my goggles. Forced to shut my eyes tight, I could only imagine what a distraction Le Petite Frenchie was for poor Dr. Sicurezza. I cannot count how many times we had to redo tests due to his interference. Dr. Intesa Sicurezza was good natured about it. Oh, how we joked about the afternoon when she—lured away by Le Petite Frenchie—forgot the blower was running on low volume and returned the next morning to find me still strapped to this stainless-steel table, nearly buried by the all-night blizzard of alabaster.

"I was positive you had left me for dead, Doctor," I said. I longed to pinch her, in all violation of lab protocol.

"Jerome, I would never kill you," Dr. Intesa Sicurezza said. "Then I would go to the prison. Or worse, face the capitalist punishment."

Her good—and sometimes trashy—humor, and adorable and broken English carried us through many a dark day in this laboratory. Who can forget the Gulliver Episode? For four eternal months our experiments stopped while government inspectors nosed around on a spurious tip that we had run tests on animals without proper certification. These were the sorts of small-minded rumors our small-minded competitors spread. Envy is a green-eyed chimera that knows no master, not even scientific reason. During those months, Intesa suffered a near breakdown that necessitated a leave of absence. Where she went, I do not know. Who consoled her, I do not know. What went through her brilliant mind, I do not know. How she survived, I do not doubt was a miracle. Needless to say, Le Petite Frenchie stopped coming around during those months, and thank goodness. Although I was distraught, I was at least free to focus on chaperoning the federal apes from Washington, whose extraordinary curiosity paled in comparison to their extraordinary ignorance. They insisted I show them every inch of space inside the facility and out, including the area behind the lab, namely the dumpster.

The rollup door at the back of our laboratory seemed to have been welded shut. The inspectors gleefully deployed crowbars. They seemed to have arrived armed with these brute tools and wedged five of them between the floor and the base of the door and pried it open in a matter of minutes. With the door rolled to the ceiling, it was there in the dumpster, sadly, that we found a lifeless and petrified form, which these inspectors mistook for Dr. Sicurezza's lost poodle. Try as I might to convince them of their misguided conclusions, it was all too clear that someone—likely Dr. Kierkenes—had brainwashed them into believing they had found Gulliver, a standard poodle and standard victim of someone's sinister and substandard science project.

"I've tried to warn you, Jerome, there are many fish in the sea, and you're cavorting with a piranha," Kierkenes whispered in my ear as we watched six inspectors in hazmat suits struggle to lift the mummified K-9 carcass from the trash bin.

With the discovery of a victim, no matter the species, these inspectors metastasized. They went from a handful of inept and innocuous inspectors to platoons of preordained persecutors who would not listen to logic. In their buttery, Bachelor-of-Arts brains, a dead animal was, as they say in the vernacular, a smoking gun. They gave me an ultimatum. Close down the research laboratory and serve three years in prison, or—scoundrels!—pay a sizable fine. All because a trash bin behind our facility, and readily accessible to anyone, contained a four-legged carcass that weighed 228 pounds. I did my best to assure them that Gulliver was at a high desert retreat with his loving master, the soon-to-be-famous Dr. Intesa Sicurezza. We all know that once planted, circumstantial evidence in the muddy minds of buffoons and bureaucrats is near impossible to eradicate, and so I paid their outlandish fine. I also implemented a series of unnecessary changes in lab protocol, which the news industry deemed newsworthy. Finally, to close this chapter, I sent a letter of protest to the appropriate government entities to ensure a record would exist of this harassment in the event another herd of taxpayer-sponsored hooligans descended on our laboratory.

A few short days after the matter was settled, Dr. Intesa Sicurezza appeared, refreshed and eager to complete the quest to, as she put it, "Turn a grown man to stone."

Her enthusiasm felt more infectious than ever. My devotion to her success more profound. Her energy—dare I say passion?—combined with the rigor of her thought processes excited my mind in new ways. Thoughts wholly unscientific entered the equation. What might we do, the two of us, once our experiment succeeded? Her time away did her good. She had allowed her hair to return to its natural jet black from the bleach blond. Both colors provided a stunning contrast to her blue eyes. She was tanned. Tanned from head to toe. Tanned, I confess, in those regions beyond the realm of lab protocol.

Alas, the news spread quickly through the research park and lunch crowd at Napoleon's BBQ that Dr. Intesa Sicurezza was back. And, Le Petite Frenchie came knocking. He wore a blue suit, pants with a tight and short European cut, shoes with long, pointed toes, his hair had a sheen to it like fresh asphalt. He stepped into the dimly lit lab uninvited. I had just unrolled a poster-sized blueprint of our newest process. The doctor in a low-cut blouse and I hunched together over the diagram. It was one of those magical nights when science's sensual side effects permeate the air like a beautiful poison. The intimate fragrance of Dr. Sicurezza's skin mingled with cement dust and the pungent scent of the damp ink on the drawing of our creation. My creative juices flowed, and my ears hummed from the blowers and fans that had roared all day. My throat burned, my eyes burned, and, naturally, my heart burned, too. We were closer than ever.

"Jerome, I have confided in you many times."

"Yes, Doctor, you know I am your faithful manservant," I shouted against the ringing in my head.

"It is time to bet the farmer."

"The farm," I corrected gently.

"Yes, let's bet the farm," she said. "Tonight, we will do it."

"I am your immortal Old McDonald," I quipped, and she patted my cheek approvingly. An electric charge snaked through every part of my physical being. If the male body truly has thirty appendages—and I am no biologist—then the hopeful caress in that moment of Intesa Sicurezza sent a tingle through all thirty of mine plus one.

"We will go and deeper," she whispered. "Tonight is the night. The risk is high, but the rewards will be immeasurable."

"To labor by your side is reward enough for me," I warbled and nudged closer so our hips rubbed, mirroring my verbiage. Then added, "Yes, deeper, deeper."

Like a sorceress, she made a pencil appear from out of her thick black hair and began to scratch novel and brilliant calculations across the blueprint—heavier volumes, higher particulate-to-moisture ratios, increased air pressure, doubled densities, hotter temperatures, longer exposure times, added electrical current. Every imaginable variable, she pushed to capacity. With each engorged factor, I heard the echo of her logic—"go and deeper, go and deeper, go and deeper, and deeper, and deeper..."

As I watched her long, firm thumbs squeeze the numbers and functions on her Texas Instruments calculator, I leaned closer. Our arms entwined innocently, I breathed in her dark hair, felt her breasts rise and fall, and the front door slammed. There he stood, Le Petite Frenchie—in one hand a single white carnation and the other two stemmed glasses and a wine bottle as open as his fly.

"Out! Out! Out of Dr. Sicurezza's laboratory this second," I yelled.

"A petite flor can do no harm," he said with a grin. It was apparent from his dress and demeanor that he was un petite intoxicated. I was certain the Doctor would not stand for it.

"Out, you rapscallion!"

"Please, Jerome, S'il vous plaît, Jerome," he said, using his facility with Romance languages to undermine me in the eyes of the Doctor. "In all these years, you have not changed. You are working too hard."

"I am relaxed. And I am not working too hard. I work as hard as is necessary for a researcher passionate about going deeper to find answers."

"Tomorrow, find answers. Then, you will be happy."

We might have come to blows if Dr. Sicurezza had not intervened. Taking my hand, she asked that I run to the hardware store to purchase the necessary materials for our final experiment. I could not refuse her. Yet, as I strolled the fluorescent aisles of the 24-hour home supplies store, I tried—

for the first time—to not imagine the doctor.

When I returned two hours later, Le Petite Frenchie was nowhere in sight. I confessed to Dr. Sicurezza that I had wandered the aisles aimlessly for almost an hour and made a wrong turn on the drive back to the lab.

"It is to be expected. Disorientation is a standard emotion in a moment of conquest," she said as she cinched the orange nylon straps across my chest for the last time. This stainless-steel table where I had lain comfortably dozens of times now felt icy and my entire body shivered for the first time. I shut my eyes while Intesa fitted the goggles tight to my forehead and cheeks.

"May I ask a favor of you, Intesa?" I said, my voice trembling with excitement, anticipation, fear.

"Anything, my little man," she said.

"Please, remove the goggles."

"But, there is no time."

"Just for a moment," I pleaded.

I looked into Intesa Sicurezza's ingenious blue eyes for what I feared might be the last time. I am in no condition to define what I saw, but one might describe it as alarm. And so I said the second thing that was on my mind.

"So that my goggles don't fog over and I can see to the very last moment," I asked, "please would you spit on my mask for me."

As I lay here now, in my current state and future state, I confess. No, there is no excitement in the knowledge that this day brings the publication of our results. Morning has arrived. The roll-up door in this warehouse has never quite reached the floor, ever since the inspectors took their crowbars to it. Now, I hold my gaze on the bright white line that radiates between the door and the concrete floor—this light, the sign that morning has broken. They say when one dies an incendiary light appears that you move toward and ultimately through. I don't believe that phenomenon has been proven as a fact, but I do believe in death. This bright bead of sunlight reminds me of it—as if one of my more brilliant neighbors has encapsulated the essence of the ever-after and reconstituted this portal as a band of blinding pearly light. Each morning, it comes to me. I've watched it appear day after day. Yes, I am always awake. I wonder if Dr. Intesa Sicurezza vanished through that light. I have not seen her or heard from her in weeks. Only my friend Hand Kierkenes visits me, and feeds me, and tells me the latest news and shares with me his stories, which I know are lies. That white light gives me a strange secular hope. I don't know if such a reformulation is possible, but were I someday, somehow, somewhere to regain the use of my body, this is the research I would pursue. I would prove that the unfathomable radiance that we imagine and fear, can be stretched and flattened under certain controlled conditions into a mystical wand. Maybe my hypothesis is flawed, but I do believe we humans have an innate ability to transform anything we want into a phenomenon that we will never comprehend.

The Man Playing Violin

thomas hedt

From the street corner
vibrations sent
through grain of spruce
golden   tight
sharp as   knives
tuned   to an   echo

bring forward no heirlooms
no jewelry   cufflinks   combs
only that which is coded
as if fingers were still tapping
copper keys in the mud
of a bunker

bring forward only
that which is carried
ageless in psyche and dream
carry me onward
as if I were   an echo
not yet born

Sgaile: The Art of Making Poisons Pleasant
phillip hurst

"No," my girlfriend Sara said, "the Bible is *not* just another book."

Sensing this conversation could be sidestepped no longer, I'd snuck a couple whiskies before clocking out of the restaurant where we both worked. Turns out, however, the lubricated tongue isn't always the wisest of tongues.

"Faith is real to me," Sara said, "and it's real to my family, to the people I love. Don't you get that?"

I said, of course, sure—but I didn't get it, not really. We were in the mossy woods just past the employee parking area, near a glittering spot that later served as backdrop for a Hollywood blockbuster about lovestruck teenage vampires. Sara sat atop a slab of quarried granite festooned with lichen. On the way, ever the Boy Scout, I'd pit-stopped at my Honda for a fresh bottle of Oban. Now I took a courageous pull, swishing the lush whisky around my tongue: rich barley, tangerine, a hint of peaty smoke. I offered Sara the bottle.

"Thanks, but I actually want to feel this."

"To each their own."

"You poison yourself with that stuff so you never have to really feel anything. You realize that, right?"

I shrugged and took a drink for the both of us.

While there was a dose of truth in Sara's observation, single malt was a spirit I actually did put considerable faith in. Moreover, scotch and agnosticism have something of a history together.

But first, by way of background, consider *A Journey to the Western Islands of Scotland* (1775), which records the travels of Dr. Samuel Johnson while he traipsed the Hebrides with his faithful biographer, James Boswell. Being a Scotsman himself, Boswell couldn't help but have some fluency in the language of his homeland's native spirit, whereas Dr. Johnson was a tea-drinking Englishman who dismissed scotch whisky as, "the art of making poison pleasant."

Also of note is a peculiar local term—*sgaile*—which according to MacLeod's dictionary can mean, "a smart knock or blow" (to the head, presumably, as the term also connotes baldness), as well as, "a bumper of any spirituous liquor taken before breakfast."

Read together then, these definitions suggest Johnson and Boswell just may have stumbled upon an eighteenth-century Scots Gaelic reference to a practice more modernly known as "the hair of the dog."

In 1776, however, just a year after their travelogue appeared, Boswell paid a visit to another famous writer and Scotsman—the philosopher David Hume. Boswell hadn't called upon his countryman to talk hangover cures, though. Instead, he'd come to Hume on his deathbed, wondering whether the renowned unbeliever—by that point "lean, ghastly, and quite of an earthy appearance"—might like to recant a lifetime of public heresy before it was too late. What were a few quick words of repentance, after all, compared to the soul's writhing in eternal fire?

Whether Boswell had the courtesy to bring along a bottle on this errand is not recorded, but like the deathbed conversion he'd sought, single malt is sometimes "finished" in a second vessel—sherry casks, American oak, wine foudres—and this process can be thought of (assuming one doesn't mind stretching a metaphor) as a last chance to make amends for a spirit's intrinsic faults, to smooth over all those troublesome original sins. Hume was a genuine iconoclast, though, a man who'd spent a lifetime thinking through his rationalism and materialism. So he ultimately took a pass on Boswell's offer, the reaper on the stoop be damned.

Being of devout mind, Boswell was deeply troubled by Hume's nonchalance in the face of mortality, so much so that he later mentioned the incident to his friend and muse, the pious Dr. Johnson (whom Boswell describes as always having had an intense "horrour of death"), but the doctor merely scoffed and claimed Hume only feigned indifference to the New Testament out of intellectual vanity. Nonetheless, Hume's ease in the face of his own imminent dissolution left poor Boswell disturbed for some time—if not even, dare I say, sgailced.

Hoping to forestall the imminent dissolution of our relationship, I again offered Sara the Oban.

While this time she took a polite sip, she was right: the scotch wasn't helping with the comeuppance of our differences. We really did care for one another, though. Before we'd even gotten together, there'd been months of lingering eye contact and friendly-but-flirty banter, Sara posted up by the bar rolling silverware in a stack of green linens while I polished the same three wine glasses over and over again. Being so vibrant and pretty, however, Sara had of course been encumbered by a meddlesome boyfriend, whom it'd taken some time to outfox, although outfox him I ultimately did. I distinctly recall the moment the tides turned.

It was a drizzly morning and I was in the basement gathering bottles to restock when Sara floated down the uneven wooden stairs. There was no reason for her to be in the basement and we both knew it. We looked at one another across the crated beer and wine and I felt again that Sara was someone I might genuinely connect with. She was an artist, a maker of jewelry and paintings who peddled her works at the downtown Saturday Market and spoke of someday attending art school. She was as eclectic as she was desirable, fun-loving and open-hearted and easy to talk with in a way that's rare—or at least rare for a shy person like myself.

Jangling silverware and creaking footsteps echoed down from the dining room. The lunch rush would be upon us any minute, but for now the liquor room was ours alone. We stood just a step apart. I might have kissed her then, despite the boyfriend. There was a moment when it would've been right.

"What's this?" Sara finally asked, her hand rising to my throat. Then she unbuttoned my shirt collar and reached inside, her fingers brushing the skin of my chest. She lifted out the piece of metal I wore on a cord around my neck and studied the mass-produced and characterless jewelry. Then she looked me flush in the face and said, "I can make you a better one."

After she'd gone, I took a deep breath and picked up the stacked boxes of liquor and wine. Hard to see with the bottles pressed under my chin, but I took my time and was almost back up to the restaurant when—daydreaming about that lost kiss—my foot slipped. I barked my shin and banged into the wall. My attempts to save the leaning tower of booze resulted in a graceless half-turn, a yelp, and a fall. Both cases spilled. Tequila and scotch and a veritable host of wine bottles rained down the stairs, somersaulting and clattering, breaking and spraying the walls and floor amidst a breathtaking racket.

It wasn't long before another sort of fall occurred, though. But sometimes even that still isn't enough. Because besides matters religious, the months to come revealed other differences. I was interested in writing, for one thing, whereas literature didn't always pique Sara's interest. I wanted to spend more time in the city, and yet she was thinking of leasing a cabin in the woods. Did I want to live out there with her? If not, what was I waiting for—for some other girl, a more bookish and intellectual girl, to come along? The sum of these differences had, without either of us quite realizing it, sickened our tender relationship.

When Sara began to cry, I plucked the Oban from her hands.

"Please stop," I said, and took another, deeper drink. "I'm sorry."

Her tears flowed so gracefully. That's what I remember best. No hitching breath, no grimacing, no splotchy skin. Just those clean tears gliding down the planes of her face. Unsure what else to say, I offered to start attending church.

"It's not just about going to church," Sara said. "It's about how you feel inside."

Hearing her impassioned tone, it occurred that a dayshift bartender with a swollen liver had little hope of competing with the warm bosom of familial approval and the good graces of community, let alone the promise of bodiless immortality. I thought of David Hume, and how despite my tendency to play the Doubting Thomas, I probably wouldn't be quite so stoic on my own deathbed. How I'd almost certainly lose my nerve and call out for salvation, spiritual or otherwise—call out, that is, to the very deity who was at that moment looking down in mirth, His having outfoxed me to the tune of one lovely girlfriend.

I thought a little sentimentality might smooth things over, a last-ditch jaunt down memory lane. "Remember our first date?"

"Of course, I do," Sara said.

I smiled. "It was pretty trippy, I guess."

"It was more than that," she said. "You know it was."

And Sara was right again, as our relationship had been colored by the otherworldly from the very beginning. That first date took place not long after the tumble I'd taken down the stairs. We both had Sunday off, and decided to hike the Columbia River Gorge and see some waterfalls. Driving along the winding and picturesque historic highway, the good clean smell of the forest whipped through the cab and a few stray wisps of blonde hair danced around Sara's face. I could hardly keep my eyes on the road. Once parked at the trailhead, however, we both studied the baggie of dirty little mushrooms in her lap.

I asked if they were safe.

"They're from the earth," she said.

Spoken like a true Flower Child. A cook we worked with had mentioned having procured a particularly groovy batch, and while said cook didn't strike me as a trustworthy sort (all the kitchen guys seemed vaguely criminal), 'shrooming with Sara in the Gorge sounded like fun.

Still, we were both nervous. Such fungi were illegal, after all, although the criminalization of their magic isn't really about public safety, as the powers that be would have us believe. Instead, it's more about the manner in which they encroach upon the spiritual realm—that sacred trinity which the philosopher-statesman Thomas Paine (who in 1776, the year of Hume's death, would publish Common Sense and rally the revolution) aptly christens, "mystery, miracle, and prophecy."

Sara didn't seem overly concerned about illegality or the prospect of sinning, though, and so we gobbled the little suckers down and hit the trail.

Half an hour later, passing through a gorgeous stretch of old growth forest, I was sure that cook had swindled us. But then a slight nausea. The feeling worsened, my stomach twisting, but just when it seemed I'd be sick in front of my date, a glorious sweat broke from my every pore and the illness lifted. That, or I was simply distracted by the curious way the cedar chips had begun forming mosaics underfoot…which, upon my noticing them, shifted into whorled triskele and sand mandala, before unspooling and coalescing into other, stranger shapes.

I felt unusually present in my skin—a skin no longer of its accustomed seeming, my arms covered in patches of burning red freckles like islands on a map or constellations in the nighttime sky—and it occurred that this body of mine was so very strange, not a possession, not a thing I had but what I *was*…an envelope of flesh that would soon enough sink back into the earth, decaying and wet, like my beloved peat.

Sara hiked up ahead, a halo of light spilling from her limbs and hair. The leaves alongside the path undulated as if undersea, rubbing their mesmeric skins together and whispering secrets in our wake. How could there not be some design in this forest? The sunlight and water, the crunching cinders, the rich smell of earth and all those silent trees trading us breath for precious breath—this couldn't all be *accident*, could it? Just chemistry, chance, and eons? At that moment, the notion seemed utterly laughable. A ruse, like the voices of birds.

On this point, Thomas Paine noted that the individual who perceives the universe (soberly, he means, in both senses of the word) and yet still believes himself chosen for special significance within it, holds two hopelessly opposed thoughts in his head. Sort of the cosmological equivalent to Keats's famous line about negative capability. And just then—paused mid-step on the trail—I felt mysteriously compelled to announce (not to Sara, but to the enchanted forest itself) that I'd finally grasped Paine's misapprehension.

Sara turned around then and asked if I was okay, to which I replied that it seemed possible my thoughts may have somehow gotten spoken aloud…

But she just smiled and resumed hiking. Floating along behind her, though, the proof of Paine's error insisted upon itself. I almost had it, the ragged edges of the contradiction or paradox or whatever it was. But then the mountainous impossibility of such thoughts buried me in uncertainties and doubts and I realized I'd been staring down at my feet for an awfully long time, admiring their ridiculous size and flipper-like evolution—until a sound from the trail ahead yanked me back to what passed for reality. Not the chorus of birds or susurrus leaves, but a gathering menace: a quaking sense of imminent predation and impending doom.

I'd just begun to wonder if I'd perhaps not poisoned myself with one too many magical mushrooms when the hominid rounded a bend and loped straight at me. A Sasquatchian grotesque, nude or skinned or worse, it thundered down the trail on bristly knees, hands swinging like meathooks, its face twisted into a panting grimace of spittle-flecked incisors.

With a hoot of despair, I flung myself into a bed of ferns.

But then Sara was with me, rubbing me down like a spooked horse. *Trail runner*, she kept saying, *just a trail runner*, until we both succumbed to a bout of mad giggles.

Later, we reached trail's end. In the way of waterfalls, one led to the next and we followed a tumbling creek deep into the forest. Immaculate light lanced the canyon walls and a towering silence rose around us, much as the gothic cedars rose over the water—water that slipped over the mossy shelf to tumble and break in a ghostly spray upon boulders like the skulls of whales. Without a word, Sara stepped into the glacial stream. Up past her boots and near the edge she went, daring the slick bed and the falls. She glanced back at where I sat upon a red log gone soft in the forest's humid palm, and then in one graceful motion she peeled down her shorts and squatted. It was that oldest of human poses, African and primordial, her golden hair spilling down to the globes of her bare rump like a vision for the trail to Damascus. In the rich sunlight, her urine coruscated with all the brilliance of stained glass, braiding with the snowmelt and washing over the falls on its way to the Columbia and finally the Pacific. Then she rose and beckoned me to her, and I couldn't help but gasp when the icy waters baptized my naked and bug-bitten ankles.

"Sara, I'm sorry, but don't you ever think maybe all that stuff is just …"

The piece of jewelry she'd made for me—a dab of pewter and sliver of shell on a cord—knocked gently against the divot in my throat.

"Just what?"

Our conversation had only gotten worse: that is, gotten closer to the sort of honesty you can't really come back from.

"Never mind, I—"

"No, say what you actually mean for once."

Again, it was her tone, or something in her tone, an implication of un-certainty or even cowardice on my part, which (along with half a bottle of Oban) finally pushed me over the slippery edge. Sara wasn't trying to save me, I don't think; hers wasn't the patronizing attitude James Boswell took with David Hume, and yet she nonetheless spoke with a certainty I could not grasp. I understood that she'd armored herself against the unknowable in a fashion not so altogether different from my drinking and reading, but how could anyone be so sure of a future state, of mystery and miracle and prophecy?

More to the point, how do two peoples' beliefs about the abstract and unprovable come to poison their here and now? What was the good of agnosticism, after all—let alone books written by men like Hume and Thomas Paine, which tend to leave the honest reader with no choice but agnosticism—if the unbeliever still finds himself bereft of answers and with no way of circumventing the various dogma, religious or otherwise, that hamstring one's chances for tranquility in a godless world brimming over with godly friends and lovers?

Sick with frustration and already dreading the return of the old loneli-ness, I heard my voice as if coming from another's throat, using phrases like *wish-thinking* and *spiritual gobbledygook* and calmly but insistently pepper-ing Sara with questions we both knew she couldn't answer, because they were the sort of questions human beings aren't meant to answer, which is to say I was being immature and unfair at best, if not flatly cruel—although to whom that cruelty was actually directed now feels harder to say.

In the silence to follow, Sara hopped down from the slab of granite and the hurt and raw look on her face had me backtracking and claiming I'd misspoken, that I hadn't meant those things the way they'd sounded, that I was sorry, that it was just the whisky talking.

When still she didn't speak, I dropped the Oban in the weeds, took her face in my hands, and kissed her. Our first kiss had been magical—

in a 'shroomy sort of way and a lovestruck Hollywood sort of way—but much like the sequels to those teenybopper vampire flicks, this last kiss felt strained. And Sara apparently felt the same way, because after the briefest taste of salt and whisky on her plump bottom lip, she recoiled from my smoky breath and looked at me in shock—almost as if (instead of rakish fangs) I'd sprung horns and a pointy red tail.

Then she spun on the heels of her nonslip shoes and walked away.

From that greenly eerie pocket in the trees, I heard her old primer gray Chevy cough to life. Then tires spitting gravel. Between my feet lay the bottle. But upon kneeling to retrieve it, I grimaced against a sudden ache in my skull, a bolt of pain just behind the eyes in that mysterious place where one almost cannot help but feel as if the soul must reside.

fiction

Dysphagia
simon nagel

Doc had been chewing for over a minute and dreaded what came next, but he had to eat. His throat pulsated, pushing the mash up and down against the sides of his esophagus until it finished the long slog into his stomach. He took a breath and his eyes watered as the crisp air swept through his windpipe. He wiped his eyes and checked to see if anyone was staring at him. Breakfast was a gauntlet Doc passed with less confidence every morning. He knew the day his gag reflex returned would be the end of his time on the road.

He typed the same tired Facebook update into his phone. It had been a great run of shows all week, and he would be available for pictures at the Waffle House before his final performance. It received two likes while he waited for anyone to come by. A waitress asked if he wanted anything to go with his banana. Doc told her he was fine, thank you.

Doc fondly recalled fairgrounds dusted with fallen leaves and ticket stubs, but throughout the years those mainstays had given way to discarded Cheeto bags and half-eaten funnel cakes. He chalked it up to a sign of the times as he hoisted his knife kit from the back of his Toyota Tercel. He was saddened by how deeply the trunk pressed into the softness of his stomach as he hauled it across the fairgrounds. It was a fact he had wanted to deny for many years, but the demands of the road put him in front of too many things deep fried and convenient. Doc laid out his knives inside the performance tent and pondered what his days would be like after retirement. He didn't exactly have a home to go back to where he could plan his next move.

A kid wearing a paint-splattered jacket motioned to Doc from the stage as the audience in attendance gazed in his direction. They reminded Doc of a bunch of cattle in a field somewhere, chewing on cud as the day passed. He began reciting his introductory statement without waiting for any applause. He had long foregone adding anything new to his routine. No jokes were necessary. He'd give the length and dimension of the blade in hand before shoving it down his throat and continue the process until it was time to cock his head back and safely drive a nail through his nose and down his nasal passage in a grand finale. He coasted through the performance, stealing glances at the vacant, gaping faces in the audience. They gave tepid applause that seemed to grow softer after each blade. It stirred up a memory of the old hand-carved oak sign from his earliest gig, back in the days when they were known as "Curiosity Galleries." The sign told them to gaze upon a cabinet of splendor and complexity, and they poured into the tent to be shown the extraordinary. The room would be in such awe, so much wonder of Doc's ability that the only sound anyone would hear was the slow creaking of the sign back and forth. It had been a long time since Doc had heard that kind of quiet. Now the children were bathed in the blue light of their phones and the adults were numbed by hours of never-ending buzzer sounds. Doc eyed the final blade in the bottom of his trunk, his widest and deepest. His world-record sword with its beautiful one hundred and twenty-degree curve. He pulled the nail out of his nostril and closed the trunk. The crowd didn't deserve that sword. They hadn't for years.

Doc's phone was running out of power by the time he managed to find his tenth-grade crush on Facebook. He was sitting at the food truck outside the fairgrounds, idly seeking her out while he ate. She had the same face but had gone through the wear and tear of giving birth to four children. He enlarged the picture until her chin was cut off and basked in the close-up. Doc pressed his last french fry into a plastic cup full of ranch before shoving it in his mouth. It slid down his throat, leaving a soothing trail that made him forget about the lump it left in his stomach. The phone went dead and it was time to go back to the motel.

It took a few tries to get the Tercel's engine going. The A/C had died in the summer, so Doc drove with the windows cracked, even though the temperature was starting to dip. He drove in silence to the Motel 6, wondering if he should take the scenic route to the last fair of the season in Wichita Falls.

It was too early to go to sleep. Doc had made a rule a long time ago that he would never drink by himself in a motel room. He rubbed his throat and took the ice bucket down to the soda machine. The ice maker was out of order, so Doc settled for two packs of Rolos and a Slim Jim. He continued down the hall, feeling the night air pass through his T-shirt. He reached the motel lobby and glanced inside, hoping for a confirmation that he wasn't entirely alone.

She was hovering near the travel brochures, drinking burnt coffee from a Styrofoam cup while she waited for the desk clerk to bring out the continental breakfast whenever 5 a.m. finally rolled around. She wore red and brown striped socks to the tops of her calves, making her legs look like chocolate candy canes. She caught Doc looking at her and shifted away, revealing a webbed tattoo on the soft tuffet of skin between her Adam's apple and her chin. Doc breathed through his nose nervously and resisted the urge to avert his gaze. His thighs quivered and he weaved back and forth, but Doc figured he had more highway behind him than in front of him. It was a night to be bold. He carried that thought with him as he walked inside and asked if she wanted to join him at the soda machine.

"I was just there. There's some nice stuff." It felt like a decent thing to say. Doc worried that his long time on the road made him come off as desperate but it was too late now. Besides, she already said yes.

They sat on his bed eating their finds from the vending machine. Tears welled in Doc's eyes as he forced the Rolo down without his usual marathon of chewing. He pretended to sneeze so he could wipe his eyes. She could never know. Not so soon. She was working on her Hostess Snowball when she introduced herself as Nell, short for Cornelia.

"How'd you get the name Doc?"

"I was always running around with knives as a kid. Everyone just figured I wanted to be a doctor." It's true. They did. And Doc did love playing with knives as a boy, but never to cut into anyone for surgery. The very thought of it nearly brought back his gag reflex. His dreams were found in the juggling, card tricks and graphics on the back of comics showing savages from the Pacific Islands swallowing blades of fire. They became heroes to the boy from the small ranch in backwoods Oregon. He only bled the first time he swallowed a kitchen knife and gagged for just a moment when he swallowed an old sprinkler pipe he found in his father's shed. He started performing wherever he could and eventually his real life began as an entertainer in Curiosity Galleries. The look on Nell's face as he revealed himself reminded Doc of how the audiences used to look at him while he performed. He asked if she would like to see him swallow a sword. Her toes curled beneath her striped socks before she said yes, and Doc knew which sword he had to use.

He brushed the thin layer of dust off the sword of swords, the one that put him in the record books. In that way Doc would live forever, but this feat felt more precarious than anything else that had come before. He had never swallowed for a woman. He gave his introduction with a slight flutter in his voice and a flair of showmanship that made Nell lean across the bed in anticipation. She put the Snowball on the bedside ashtray and rested her hands in her palms as she lay on her stomach. Doc's grip tightened on the hilt. He would have to insert the sword at an angle and feel his way down, adjusting to the curve the deeper he went. His arms ached from holding such a large blade high above his head and he felt out of practice, but he had to go on. Nell kicked her feet back and forth like a child when he made his first adjustment. He felt her excitement as the sword passed through his chest cavity and Doc felt his heart thumping against the blade. The tip had made it to his stomach and his palms were clammy. He arched his back for the sword's curve. Doc slowly removed his hands and outstretched them to the sides, bearing himself for Nell. He and the blade, flesh and steel, were made one for this night. He only wished he could have seen her past the hilt. He heard the bed creak as she rolled out of it. Doc wanted to turn to her, but he kept his hands out for an embrace. His body quaked. As much as he cherished the moment, he couldn't take it for much longer. All he heard next was the thrashing of clothes and a thud from his trunk. He finally caught a glimpse of Nell through the changing mirror as she ripped his wallet from his pants pocket and took a pearl-handled dagger from the trunk before leaping over the bed and bounding out the door into the night. Doc stood in the center of his motel room as his heart broke with the sword still inside him. It was several minutes before he took it out.

Doc pawned the rest of his swords the next morning. He took the pawn broker's consignment note and lumbered back to the Tercel. Something stopped him before he began the increasingly long ritual of starting the engine. It was a thought behind a thought, and the only way to get to it was through wistfulness. He thought of the shows he had performed and wondered about all of his skills and joys and late-night jokes. They were moments that had gone from being so lush and wild but somehow had brittled and fallen away like autumn leaves. There was a town just beyond Wichita Falls that he drove by every year but never visited. It had a small bridge going over a brook and a main street drag where everyone in town saw each other every day. At least, that was the impression it left in the rear-view mirror. It had no fair to speak of and looked like it belonged in the oil paintings of nice little towns that adorned faded walls of old motel rooms. Doc's throat prickled as he smiled. He got the engine going on the first try.

poem

Exchange
edythe haendel schwartz

Mercado, Salta, Argentina

Vendors set their wares on makeshift shelves
before *Hotel Solar de la Plaza*,
cry *urna funeraria, antiquedades.*

Bone ash clings to emptied urns, to names
scored in Cacán, tongue crushed
under Spanish thumb.

The law protects antiquities
our tour guide says
*but Diagita claim the burial grounds
as theirs, exhume the urns.
A family can live a year
on what collectors pay.*

No raindrops puncture dust.
The stolen dead stand stacked.
Ancestral voices crackle from clay tongues,

each exchange, double edged.
Children stare from ochre arches,
run to us with outstretched hands

Your Social

bronwyn mauldin

Need has a way of sneaking up on you with its puffy eyes and scrawny neck. Things get worse and you adjust, thinking you're pretty clever to have figured a way through. Then they get worse again, and one day you discover life has become unbearable.

"Name?" the clerk asked.

"Lilian Martinez."

"Home address?"

Lilian gave her grandma's apartment. It was the closest thing she had to a home these days.

"Social?"

Lilian rattled off the eleven digits.

The clerk shook his head without looking away from his screen. "That's government. I need your handle."

"My handle?"

"What you call yourself online."

"Online?"

He made an odd clucking sound in the back of his throat and pointed at the cell phone on his desk. Lilian stared at it, trying to guess at what he wanted. Whatever it was, she'd probably do it. She looked up at him. The expression on the clerk's face was a hopeful half-smile under droopy eyes, like a well-trained cocker spaniel that knows better than to beg but wishes all the same.

"Your social media handle."

"I don't have one."

"Ha-ha," the clerk said in a flat voice. "I only need one."

"I don't use social media."

"Where did you post selfies when you graduated high school?"

"I didn't."

The clerk cocked his head, ever more puppyish. "You didn't?"

"I was home schooled."

"Where do you announce relationship changes?"

"I'm telling you, I don't have any social media."

He picked up a spiral bound notebook with a purple and pale green cover and flipped through it: *Administrator's Guide to Basic Income*. "Aha!" he said. "How many followers do you have?"

"None that I know of." It was all she could do not to make a show of turning around as if to look for anyone lurking behind her. She knew what he meant, and it was beginning to make her angry.

"What was the hashtag your parents created for you when you were born?"

"They didn't."

He ran his finger down the page.

"What is your personal brand or logo?"

"Why would I have a logo?"

"To sell stuff online."

"I don't."

The clerk flipped to the next page and read a few lines to himself. He slapped the notebook shut and dropped it on his desk, then leaned forward and poked Lilian's shoulder with two fingers.

"Ouch! What the hell was that for?"

"Checking to make sure you're not a hologram."

"I'm not."

"No, you're not."

Lilian rubbed her shoulder. It didn't hurt so much as she felt insulted. "I'm a human being and I'm trying to sign up for Basic."

The clerk swiveled his chair and folded his hands across his belly. "I don't think I can help you."

"I thought this was the Basic Income office."

"It is."

"And everybody's eligible for Basic. *You've earned it simply by being alive,*" she recited.

"Correct."

"So sign me up."

"I can't. Not without proof."

"Proof of what?"

"Proof that you exist."

Lilian held out her arms. "Of course I exist. I'm sitting here right in front of you, and you've demonstrated quite clearly I'm not a hologram. So give me the paperwork or forms to sign or whatever it is I have to do."

"I'm sorry, what was that?"

"Sign me up for Basic."

"I can't. Not without proof."

Not that again. "Let me talk to your supervisor. You have to give me Basic."

"No, I don't."

"It's a government program."

"Basic Income is a public-private partnership administered by our company." He handed her a flyer in the same purple and pale green as the *Administrator's Guide.* In a chunky sans serif font it read:

Experience the joys of the Fourth Industrial Revolution!
Sign up for Basic Income today
- Receive monthly payments for life
- Live the life you were born to live
- Pursue your dreams without fear or famine
- You've earned it simply by being alive

She flipped it over and read the back.

To receive Basic Income, you must be
- An American citizen
- Residing in the United States
- At least 21 years of age
Sign up now at your local Basic Income office
Enjoy your life and let algorithms do the hard work!

Lilian placed the flyer on the desk. She had a copy of it in the small backpack at her feet, the paper soft from handling and furry at the edges. Nearly six months earlier a librarian had given it to her as he'd escorted her out of the building. She'd been sleeping nights in a little-used closet in back for weeks, tucked in amidst the cleaning supplies. She'd begun to hope she might make it through the winter when the librarian had caught her sneaking into her hiding place at closing time. He'd been nice about it, at least. He hadn't called security. He'd given her directions to the nearest shelter, a twenty-dollar bill from his own wallet, an apology she didn't deserve, and this flyer. The flyer was why she was here, and she couldn't figure out why this clerk was giving her a hard time. She looked at his pale white hands on the armrest of his chair. Was he on some weird race-based power trip?

"What's your name?" she asked.

The clerk smiled and sat up. "Phil."

"Okay, Phil, I don't know what a public-private partnership is—"

He broke in, "It says right here," and pointed to the small print on the back of the flyer.

Basic Income is a public-private partnership that puts private sector technology and innovation to work for you, advancing public services by increasing operational efficiency. We welcome your feedback @BasicIncome #BasicIncomeIsForEveryone

"Hashtag-basic-income-is-for-everyone," she said. "I was born in this city, I've lived here all my life, and I turned 21 yesterday. Your brochure says I'm eligible. So I'm here to sign up, like everybody else who's impatiently waiting for you to get done with me so they can enroll." She waved her arm in the direction of the people sitting in purple beanbag chairs and pale green recliners in the waiting area.

Phil's eyes and nose screwed up and he tilted his head at a slight angle. "Come again?"

Lilian felt her face getting hot. "Are you doing this on purpose, pretending like you don't understand what I'm saying? Do you think if you stare at me long enough and act stupid enough that I'll give up and walk out of here? Well I won't. I am entitled to this program like every other American, and I will sit in this chair until you sign me up."

She at least had the satisfaction of seeing Phil's face turn pale, but he still looked confused. "Could you, maybe…." Rather than finish his sentence he held his hands in front of his chest parallel to each other, and squeezed them together like a small accordion, and said, "Shorter."

Lilian was nonplussed. "Are you trying to piss me off?"

"No," Phil said.

He'd understood that, at least.

He pointed at her. "You," he said. "Like this." He squeezed his hands together again with a cluck. "Less words."

"Look, dude, I'm sitting here speaking perfectly good English, trying to sign up for Basic Income, and you, for some unfathomable reason, have decided you want to keep me from getting it, which is not cool."

Lilian heard that same strange clucking sound coming from behind her. She turned to see another clerk peering around from the next cubicle and pointing to Phil's phone. "Interpreter."

At that, he brightened and pressed a button and spoke into a speaker. Lilian heard the woman on the other end of the line answer. "Sossina speaking."

"Interpreter to cube 38."

"Language?"

"Classical, I think."

"I'll be right over."

Phil smiled at Lilian, who scowled back at him, as they waited.

Sossina arrived shortly, pushing a small gray office chair on squeaky wheels. She looked to be just a little older than Phil, who Lilian thought was probably a decade older than herself. Sossina's skin, Lilian noticed, was a few shades darker than her own. An ally? She hoped so. Sossina introduced herself to Lilian with a handshake, then shook Phil's hand. Then she sat down. "How can I help you?"

Phil said, "I can't understand her."

"No, he can understand me sometimes, but only when he wants to. I can't figure out his game. It's like he's trying to prevent me from getting Basic Income, for which I am totally, one hundred percent eligible."

Sossina smiled. "I see." She turned to the clerk. "Phil, sign her up for Basic Income." Then she made that clucking sound in her throat and pointed to Lilian.

"I know, but she doesn't exist."

"How the hell can he say I don't exist when I am sitting right here on this chair in front of him? You can see me, can't you? He damn well poked me in the shoulder, and he can tell as well as you that I am not a hologram." Lilian grabbed Sossina's hand. "See?"

"Please remove your hand from my person. We will get to the bottom of everything."

"You better do what she says," Phil said.

Lilian let go and sat back. "That puto understands you but doesn't understand me?"

Sossina pursed her lips together. "Lilian, I can help you out here, but for that to happen you must pull yourself together. I realize this kind of corporate bureaucracy can be extremely frustrating, but I cannot help if you refuse to behave like an adult."

Phil, Lilian was somewhat mollified to see, was now staring at Sossina with that same idiot puppy dog confusion in his eyes. Sossina noticed it too. She clucked and pointed to Lilian. "S'okay. Let's do it."

Phil rearranged himself in his chair, turned to his screen, and hovered his hands over his keyboard as if starting over from scratch. "Social?"

Lilian took a deep breath to keep herself from screaming, then recited the eleven digits slowly.

"See?" Phil said, pointing at Lilian and making that cluck in his throat that was starting to irritate her.

"Lilian," Sossina said, "the number you've given us is for government use only. We are not the government, as I expect he told you already. Phil is asking you to give him your social media handles."

Lilian sighed.

Sossina held up a placating hand. "It's really only necessary for you to give us one of them. We can run an algorithm that combines it with your name and cell phone number to find the rest. We'll probably even dig up a few old defunct accounts you don't remember opening."

"That's the thing. I've never used social media. My parents had a few accounts when they were young, but they closed them and scrubbed the data before I was born. They home-schooled my brother and me to keep us out of the system."

Sossina nodded. She didn't seem as surprised or confused as Phil had. He looked back and forth between the two women as they talked, a blank but hopeful expression on his face.

"Email?" Sossina asked.

"I have an account, but I don't use it much."

Phil brightened. "Email doesn't count as proof," he said with a smile.

"He understood that?" Lilian asked.

"What about college? They would have created an account for you in one of those online systems where you attended lectures, got your assignments, turned in homework, all that."

Lilian shook her head. "I didn't do college."

"Do you do some kind of work with your hands, like build or deliver? Or clean?"

"I don't do much of anything right now."

"Oh, I see. How are you surviving?'

Lilian felt something crack open in her chest. No one had asked her a question like that in a very long time. Even her grandma seemed to take for granted the bags of food she brought her every couple of weeks. There weren't many jobs you could get without a social media history. She'd thought Basic would be different. It was supposed to be for everyone. "I get by."

"How, without social?" Phil asked.

Lilian raised her hands in astonishment and opened her mouth to speak, but Sossina cut her off. "Let me explain, Lilian. He can't understand us when we say more than a sentence or two at a time. Spoken language that uses complex-compound sentences or a lot of big words, or strings together entire paragraphs in one breath, they call that 'classical English.' Most people your age don't talk like you. They talk like Phil, quick phrases and short bullet points. As for listening, after about a hundred characters or so, they shut down and can't process anything."

"But you speak classical English."

"English is my fourth language. I learned it in school when I was growing up in Eritrea. My first teacher was an American journalist living in exile. She loved the language and taught it to us the way she had learned it."

"Do you have social?"

Sossina slid her eyes at Phil then back at Lilian, which she took to be a warning. "Yes, like most Americans I have several social media handles."

"Sossina has proof," Phil chirped.

"Well, then, my question is this," Lilian began, drawing out her words as she took Sossina's warning to heart, "if you have all the social media proof they're demanding then why are you working here? You could take Basic and you wouldn't have to work at all."

"Ah, yes. I can see you're still young, and you've been brought up outside the system." Sossina smiled. "It's a little like you were raised by wolves, and I mean that in the best way. It's why you can speak classical English, which is good because you'll need that kind of persistence to survive. You see, Basic Income is just that. It's basic. It's enough for one person to survive, but to live a full life you'll want to supplement it, which means employment. You'll also need more than Basic if you have to support other people who aren't eligible. Other people who don't have proof."

Lilian understood exactly what she was hinting at. She thought about her grandma, about all struggles her family had gone through to live an analog life in a digital world. She'd thought Basic Income would overcome all of it.

As children, she and her brother hadn't been aware of what they were missing. They hadn't known that all the other kids spent most of their time in front of screens while they'd been hammering together go-carts and building lamps out of jugs and vases they'd found on curbside trash piles. They hadn't even had internet access at home. It wasn't until they were much older that they discovered their education had been limited to what their parents knew and what could be read while sitting in the library because even a library card required proof. It was easy to think of her family as a ragged wolf pack.

She turned to Phil, who still had the same uncomprehending half-smile on his face. "Why can't I get on Basic without social?"

Phil smiled. He seemed pleased to be invited back to the conversation. "We have to be able to reach you."

"I have a phone. Call me."

He shook his head. "Advertising. You have to be segmented."

Lilian raised her eyebrows. This, she knew about from her mama and papa wolf. They'd explained social media to her and her brother the day they'd stumbled upon it while hanging out with neighborhood kids. "You mean, you want my personal data so you can advertise to me."

Now Phil grinned, wide open and friendly. "Yes." He clucked and gave a thumbs up.

"If I have to give you my personal data, then Basic isn't actually free."

"We've monetized your leisure activities."

"What?"

"It's our company motto: The triple bottom line virtuous cycle."

"Triple what?"

"You live the good life, we make the money, we pay you to live." He clucked and held up both palms and waggled his fingers in the air.

"Jazz hands," Sossina interpreted.

"What's that irritating cluck sound you all keep making?"

"Shutterclick," Phil said. He clucked again and held up his thumbs and forefingers in the shape of a partial square around his face.

"That was a selfie," Sossina said. "Sometimes I fear for the future of the English language. Then I remember that languages are living constructs. As we humans and our societies evolve, some things get worse but some things get better. Today we have selfies, but we also have Basic Income."

"Sandwich?" a voice said, followed by a cluck, startling Lilian. A young white woman stood beside her holding a shiny aluminum filigree tray toward them as if presenting a precious award. Arrayed on the tray were a dozen sandwiches on small buns. The top of each bun was embossed with the company logo in a swirl of purple and pale green. The sandwiches were lined up in three rows. A slip of folded paper named each row: BBQ Chicken, Tri-Tip, Veg.

"No, thank you," Lilian and Sossina said, almost in unison. Phil snatched a chicken sandwich, held it beside his face and made a one-handed selfie gesture, clucking and winking simultaneously at the tray bearer.

"That means thank you," Sossina told Lilian while Phil bit off half the sandwich in a single bite.

Lilian watched Sossina, who watched the clerk continue down the row of cubicles, then wind through the collection of recliners and beanbag chairs in the waiting area, presenting her tray of sandwiches to each person in turn as she passed. Phil was licking barbecue sauce from his fingers when Lilian said, "I can't imagine being offered lunch at the DMV."

"We're a public-private partnership." Phil said. "We put private sector technology and innovation…"

"I know," Lilian said, cutting him off. "I understand everything now, even the sandwiches." She clucked and flicked her fingers at him dismissively. He pursed his lips and stopped talking.

Lilian turned to Sossina. "Couldn't he just use an online translation algorithm? Instead of you sitting here. I might not have social, but I use the internet sometimes. There must be software that could take my classical English and translate it into short words and grunts even Phil could understand."

"Translation is not the same as interpretation." Sossina frowned and tugged at the ends of her sleeves, evening them out against her wrists. "The truth is, the translation algorithms are only good for a few words at a time, or a phrase. At most, maybe a sentence or two. When they're used to translate an entire conversation that goes on for any meaningful length of time, well, do you know Godwin's Law?"

"No."

"No, what?" Phil piped up.

"No, sir." Lilian gave him a placating smile.

Sossina said, "The company hasn't been able to figure out how to get the racism out of its translation algorithms. It's baked in. In every conversation, there always comes a point where the algorithm spurts out a nasty racial epithet or some kind of screed against a minority group. It's usually race or ethnicity, but sometimes the algorithm goes berserk about women or a disability group, or LGBTQ identity. The company says they've put their best engineers on it."

Never take candy from strangers. Never trust an algorithm. Look both ways before you cross the street. These were the childhood rules Lilian and her brother had lived by. The day her brother had come home from a friend's house wild-eyed with a story about an amazing new phenomenon called video games, their parents had sat them both down for a long, serious talk. Machines could never be more righteous than people, their parents had explained, because they were made by people.

"We build tools dreaming we might rise above our human flaws, but it is our nature to build our flaws into our works," she said, echoing words she'd heard her mother say many times.

Phil clucked and gave a thumb's up.

Lilian looked at him in alarm. "Oh dear, he understood that. Do you think he might pick up classical from listening to us talk? I mean, despite the way he's treated me, he has to be reasonably intelligent to work in a job like this. And reasonably ambitious if he didn't want to live on Basic only."

"What you said was a hundred, maybe a hundred and ten characters. Possibly less if he didn't hear a comma where you paused mid-sentence. It would behoove you to be more loquacious if you want to be absolutely sure he doesn't understand what you are saying." Sossina glanced at Phil, then looked back at Lilian with a smile.

"It doesn't make sense. They've had translation algorithms forever. Maybe I'm unreasonably idealistic, but I find it hard to believe someone hasn't figured out how to make them work without sinking into racism."

"It's true the algorithms are better than they used to be. I've seen that much for myself in the Translation and Interpretation division. When I'm not here on the floor, they have me check their lab work. I'm fluent in seven different languages and conversant in another dozen or so, some of them quite obscure. Right now the record is fifteen exchanges before the first slur appears. The company has a kind of Turing test of getting to more than thirty exchanges without a slur."

Lilian leaned forward and poked Sossina in the shoulder.

"Ouch!"

"Just checking."

Phil said, "Sossina's not a hologram. She's worked here for years."

Sossina laughed. "Yes, but it would be just like the company to test an interpreter hologram on unsuspecting members of the public. You don't even want to know the kind of social engineering they do behind the scenes online."

"To tell you the truth, I think I do know."

Phil clucked, made a hashtag with the first two fingers of both hands, and said, "Trudat."

Lilian leaned over and poked him in the shoulder.

"Ouch!" he said.

She saw Sossina stifle a chuckle. "So," Lilian said, "is that it?"

"That's it," Phil said.

Sossina said, "What do you mean?"

"I mean, this seems like the point in our conversation where you lean in close and tell me in a low voice that you have a cousin or a friend who can solve all my problems by building a social media history for me. For a fee, of course."

Sossina held up her hands in a gesture somewhere between surrender and pushing Lilian away, but she didn't cluck. "Ah, well, you see, I do not have such a cousin or friend. If anyone did, it would be this gentleman at the keyboard here." She half-gestured in Phil's direction with her chin.

"But they exist? People who could build me a fake social history?"

"That would be illegal!" Phil squeaked. Three faint worry lines appeared on his forehead. Lilian mentally kicked herself for not paying attention to her language.

"I don't know anything about that," Sossina said. Her voice carried a warning in it.

"I don't mean to make trouble," Lilian said. "I just figured all sorts of people must come in to sign up for Basic. Someone like you must talk to people with so many different problems, you've probably learned all the angles. That's what I was thinking. I must have said enough words by now. Do I need to say any more?"

"You're fine," Sossina said. "Of course everything you say is true, but I could lose my job if I helped you in that way. More importantly, there are professional standards for interpretation that I am obliged to uphold. I have an ethical responsibility to forget what I hear, unless I believe the person I am interpreting might be a danger to herself or others."

"Sure. I see."

"Phil," Sossina said with a cluck, which got his rapt attention. "Read the company policy for no-socs. Page twelve, please."

Phil picked up the *Administrator's Guide* and flipped to page twelve. He ran his finger down the page and began moving his lips.

"Aloud," she said.

"Oh, right. *Start your social today and you may be eligible in as little as three years.*"

"You're young," Sossina said. "You have many years of eligibility ahead of you if you open a social media account now."

Phil clucked and held the notebook open toward Lilian, pointing to the bottom of the page. "Our *Social Media for Beginners* class meets every Tue and Thur."

Sossina said, her voice pitched only a little lower than before, "Keep in mind you don't have to tell the truth on social. You merely have to post enough material over a long enough period of time to build a historical record. Four or five posts a week. You can write them all on Sunday and schedule them to go live throughout the week."

Lilian grabbed her backpack from the floor and stood up.

Sossina stood too. "I'm truly sorry all I can do for you is interpret language and policy. And yet, I believe I've given you something of value. I can see it in your body language. You needed to know how the system works, even if you're going to live outside of it. I think you now have a clearer view of the challenges you face, but also a better sense of your inner strengths. It's not only classical English. I suspect you have other skills people have lost to automation along the way."

Raised by wolves? It was so true. Thinking of her parents that way made her love them a little bit more. Maybe she'd never be able to take Basic, but she had a private life. For so many years she had struggled against this gift, thinking it was a burden. How very wrong she had been.

Lilian flipped her pack onto her back. She shook Sossina's hand, and then Phil's. On her way out, she snatched two purple and pale green buns from the aluminum tray. Pausing in the doorway, she turned back for one last look. Phil and Sossina were still standing at his cubicle, watching her leave. She held up the sandwiches, one beside each cheek, and clucked good-bye.

poem

Fault Line

claire scott

a first for us
sharing a carry on
I pack two shirts for four days
you pack six just in case
negotiations rivaling Versailles
one pair of underpants for one pair of socks
I get three sweaters to your two
since yours take up more room
no need for five baseball caps
one paperback each, no cheating
with *The Odyssey* or *War and Peace*
no you don't need an electric toothbrush
your teeth won't turn black in four days
whereas I do need day cream, night cream, body lotion
foundation, concealer, face powder, blusher, lipstick,
lip liner, eye shadow, eyeliner, mascara, setting spray
inalienable rights of a woman
the quart size zip lock
stuffed with miniscule plastic containers
for sure one will spill
all over the Ambien, the Aricept, the Lipitor
your fault no your fault
I drag another suitcase from the closet

Four Letter Words

cedric yamanaka

For all too brief a while, Johann Song had been blessed with a good life. As the morning man for Hawaii's only classical music station, Johann attended wine tastings at opulent island resorts, enjoyed ahi tataki and salmon rolls with the governor at Washington Place, and read Prokofiev's Peter and the Wolf accompanied by the Honolulu Symphony. He was married to the lovely Joy Song, an adult day-care therapist. Their nine-year old son, Davy, was already considered to be one of the finest classical pianists on the island.

One Thursday afternoon, though, Davy ran through the hallway of his Manoa home with a pair of scissors and fell. The scissors punctured his heart. Davy died. After the horrible accident, Johann secretly preserved the scissors in a Ziploc bag, like evidence collected from a crime scene. Johann had once used the red-handled scissors to cut coupons out of newspapers, open envelopes, snip off the plastic tops of stubborn packets of ketchup. The sharp metal still contained the rust-colored remains of his son's blood.

Johann assumed Davy was going to use the scissors to cut out shapes from construction paper for a school homework assignment. That's what Joy had told the newspapers. And that's what the newspapers reported. But three days after the boy's funeral, Joy told Johann the truth. She had lied to the media. Their son had been cutting pictures out of a porno magazine.

"What?" said Johann, shocked. "But he is, was, only in the fourth grade."

"How do you explain this?" said Joy, opening a drawer in Davy's room. The drawer was filled with photos of naked and almost naked women clipped out of magazines. From Hollywood starlets to Sports Illustrated swimsuit models to MTV video vixens to Fredericks of Hollywood catalogues to hardcore porn magazines.

"I don't believe it," said Johann, stunned, leafing through the collection.

"It's all your fault," said Joy.

"My fault? I don't subscribe to any porno magazines. I've never watched a porno movie. I haven't even been to a strip club."

"You just don't get it. You screwed up Davy's childhood. You and your music. Davy never wanted to spend hours playing the piano. I tried to tell you. He wanted to surf, play soccer. Be like a regular kid. But you wouldn't let him."

"But the magazines. Where did he..."

"The magazines," said Joy. "Were mine."

"I love these shrimps," said the station manager, Nielsen Adams, to Johann. They were at the Hawaii Radio Broadcasters Awards Dinner at the Moana Surfrider, balancing Heinekens and tiny plates filled with cold shrimp and dim sum in their hands. "But I hate these parties. Every year it's the same thing. Everybody pretends they're happy for the winners, when they'd just as soon see them self-immolate. It's all so fake. Look how long the line is for the prime rib. Let's get some sushi."

Instead, Johann walked to the bar, ordered a Scotch, and—once again—thought about his missing wife and son.

On the one-year anniversary of their son's death, Joy disclosed her affair with a drug rep named Lars Burn. The couple eventually left the islands for Walnut Creek. After attorneys finalized the divorce papers, a shell-shocked Johann tried to return to a normal life. He attempted to get used to the lonely evenings, the tables for one, the missing spaces on the bed Joy once occupied.

Johann spent sleepless nights wondering if it was his allegiance to classical music that had claimed the life of his son. He recalled the many times he forced Davy to select piano recitals over soccer tournaments, student competitions over days at the beach.

As he stood by the bar, sipping his Scotch, a young woman performed a rousing medley of hits by the Pretenders. Dazed, Johann made his way towards the stage. A Chinese girl in a black t-shirt and leather pants fronted a five-piece band. Although she was tiny—she couldn't have been much taller than five-feet—her voice roared with the sound of a hundred thousand firecrackers. A golden cross dangled from her ear, and streaks of red highlighted her long brown hair. She was the most beautiful woman Johann had ever seen.

After the performance, Johann approached the girl, who sipped from a bottle of water.

"You are terrific," he gushed.

"Thanks, Mr. Song."

"You know who I am?" said Johann, startled.

"Of course," said the girl, moving so close to Johann that he could see a quick flash of her tongue ring. "I listen to you every morning."

Her name was Nicole Wong. She stood at the bar with Johann, nursing a Seabreeze, and asked him where he got his love for classical music. Johann explained. His mother—a piano teacher of some renown—had named him after the immortal German composer, J.S. Bach. Johann painted word portraits of the trauma he experienced growing up on Hawaiian homestead land in Waimanalo with the unfortunate name Johann.

"Johann?" the boys on the Kaiser football team cackled. "What kind of name is that?"

Still, Johann's enthusiasm for classical music—and the fact he'd work for minimum wage—eventually earned him a job at Hawaii's only classical music radio station. At first, he worked the graveyard shift—midnight to five, when only his mother was listening—but was eventually promoted to the prestigious morning-drive slot. It'd been nine years now.

Nicole said she had once been married to Dr. Hamlet Wong, the prominent Honolulu dentist. Alas, when Hamlet became involved with an Australian dental hygienist—a bunghole tart, Nicole called her—the marriage quickly fell apart.

"In the old days," reflected Nicole. "When I thought of my husband, I thought of only one four-letter word. Love. Since the divorce, every time I think of the pig, another very different four-letter word comes to mind."

"I can relate," said Johann. "My ex-wife was named Joy. People hear the word 'Joy' and they think of celebrations. Joy to the World, and all of that. For me, the word has a very different meaning now."

"Do you and Joy have any children?"

"Yes. No. Well, we had one son. But he, uh, passed away."

"Oh, I'm so sorry. Was he sick?"

"No. Davy fell on a pair of scissors while running in our hallway. He was nine-years old."

"I'm so sorry. My son is nine-years old. His name is Nicholas. He's a gifted pianist. He insists on listening to your radio show every morning."

"A pianist? My son was a pianist also."

"Really?"

"Yes," said Johann, feeling a sharp pain in his chest. "So, what do you do? I mean for a living?"

"You mean besides playing rock and roll? I work in, uh, communications."

"Oh, I see. Radio? TV?"

"Not quite."

Nicole explained that after her marriage had broken up, she had to look for a job. One day, she saw an ad in the paper that read, "Work at home. Easy $$$." She figured it was perfect. She could stay at home, take care of her son, and write rock and roll songs. Alas, her employers turned out to be a mysterious conglomerate called 1-888-HOT BODY. Working alongside luminaries such as Eliza the Parisian Fashion Model and Vivi the Milanese Diva, Nicole was dubbed Kimiko the Geisha. She took calls from lonely men and women, whispering in their ear, panting and moaning, offering the ubiquitous four-letter word.

"Of course, I'd rather be doing something else," said Nicole, shrugging. "But it's easy work. It puts food on the table. And it gives me time to do things that are really important."

"But what about your son?" said Johann, concerned. "Doesn't he…"

"Nicholas? He's too busy training to be a classical pianist. He doesn't suspect a thing."

The first time Johann met Nicole's gifted son, Nicholas, was at Orvis Auditorium. The young protégée had just astounded the audience with a stirring performance of Bach's Art of the Fugue. Johann was not sure if he was imagining things but, on stage, young Nicholas reminded him of his missing son. Something in the soft brown hair, the glint in his eyes. Johann felt like he was underwater, looking up towards the surface, and seeing Davy looking back down at him.

"Do you like my mom?" Nicholas asked Johann after the show. Nicole had stepped outside to field an urgent business call on her cellular phone.

"Yes," said Johann. "Very much."

"I like her, too," said Nicholas. "Except for one thing…"

"I know. The phone deal. That must be tough for you, Nicholas. But, you see, your mom is just, uh, trying to make a living."

"Oh, I know that. I don't mind that so much. It's just kinda goofy. The problem I have with Mom is her taste in music. For some reason, she loves rock and roll. Ugh! To me, rock is…"

"Don't tell me. Rock is a four-letter word."

"How did you know?"

Although he didn't say a word, Johann begged to differ with young Nicholas.

All of a sudden, he wanted to rock. He wanted to grow his hair long, itched to don spandex. He dreamed about slamming electric guitars into stacks of amps, fantasized about collecting panties thrown on stage by crazed groupies, wondered what it'd be like to toss a television set out of a hotel room window.

Of course, like a cross dresser, Johann never told a soul about his secret passion. The admission would threaten his job security at the station, and dramatically alter his reputation in the eyes of his erudite peers. Johann attempted, in vain, to discover a kindred spirit. There had to be someone like him who worked in the field of classical music who also thrilled at the sound of the screaming vocals of Ozzy, who played a mean-ass air guitar while listening to Van Halen, who marveled at the drum techniques of Neal Peart or Stuart Copeland. Often, as Johann sat in the soundproof broadcast booth playing Brahms and Dvorak, he secretly snuck a peak at Modern Guitar Player Magazine and imagined his young, confused son rummaging through a Hustler.

Once, Johann thought he found an ally in the person of Maestro Ludwig Stone of the Honolulu Symphony.

"Maestro," Johann said, during a morning show interview. "Do you ever listen to popular music?"

"Of course," said the Maestro.

"You do?" said Johann, surprised and pleased. "Who?"

"Oh, Gershwin, Irving Berlin, Leonard Bernstein…"

"No, no. I mean, like rock and roll."

"I do listen to some of that," said the Maestro, after a while, like he was confessing to murder.

"You do? Who? The early stuff? Led Zeppelin? Deep Purple? Aerosmith?"

"Uh, no. I do like some of the Beatles."

"Anybody else? Guns and Roses? Metallica? Nine Inch Nails?"

"Uh, no. Did I mention our upcoming Mozart concert?"

"I have a horrible confession to make," said Johann one day, unable to conceal the truth any longer. He sat with Nicole in her Makiki condominium, listening to her voluminous rock and roll CD collection. Nicholas was at a piano recital.

"Oh no," said Nicole. "Don't tell me. You've reconciled with your wife. I should've known this was gonna happen. My Dad was right. All men are scum."

"No, no. It's nothing like that. I'm a fraud. As a young man, I sang along with Puccini with tears of joy in my eyes. Now, at work, while playing selections from La Boheme, I often suppress a violent need to hit something. I once listened in ecstasy to Ravel's Bolero. Now, it's seventeen painful minutes of monotonous torture. There was a time when Wagner both excited and frightened me. Today, the only thing that moves inside of me during the Overture to Tannhauser is gas. Bach—my namesake—has become just another four-letter word."

"You're not a fraud," said Nicole, playing a Dokken CD. "But maybe you should count your blessings. You make a living surrounded by beautiful classical music. Look at me. I entertain a bunch of creepy folks with one hand on the telephone and one hand on their *da kines*."

One afternoon, the station manager called Johann into his office. Johann was worried. Had his boss caught him reading rock magazines on company time? Had he heard about his appearance at the recent Motley Crue concert? Sure enough, Nielsen Adams wore a pained look on his face, the face of the emergency room doctor who had unsuccessfully tended to his injured son.

"The station has just been sold," said the stricken Nielsen Adams. "And we all may be out of a job."

"What'll I do if I get fired?" Johann asked Nicole that afternoon, as the threat of unemployment abruptly hovered over him like the shadow of a large and overfed *honu*. "Without a job, where am I going to get the money to pay my mortgage, my health insurance, that boxed-set of Steely Dan's Greatest Hits I saw at Tower Records?"

"You'll find something," said Nicole, as her cell phone rang. "Stop worrying so much." She cleared her throat and picked up the phone. "Hello? Hello? You have reached Kimiko the Geisha. Moshi-moshi. I've been waiting for your call."

Look in his closet.

That's all Joy's letter read. It had come in the mail with a California post-mark. Johann walked into Davy's old room, still decorated with Dodger pennants, plastic bags filled with tiny toy soldiers, and a book of stamps from across the world. Really, thought Johann, it could be any boy's room. He opened the closet, filled with his son's aloha shirts, dress shirts, t-shirts. In the back of the closet was a cardboard box with the words PRIVATE written on it with blue marsh pen. Johann recognized his son's writing. Block print, the way architects write on blueprints. Johann took a deep breath and opened the box.

He found dozens of crude sketches of naked pre-pubescent and post-pubescent girls. Some lay spread eagled on beds and couches. Another girl lay on the hood of a sports car. Yet another girl walked out of the ocean, running her hands through her long hair. The drawings were now yellow with age and stained with roach crap and the broken bodies of silverfish.

"Davy," said Johann.

Johann and Nicole continued to see each other. And young Nicholas still lamented his mother's taste—or lack thereof—in music.

"Please help her, Mr. Song," said Nicholas. "Today, Mom was listening to some horrible drivel played by a Chinese rock star."

"Chinese rock star?" said Johann.

"Yeah. Some guy named Neil Young?"

"Neil Young's not Chinese. He's Canadian."

"He is? Then why is his last name Young? Is anything wrong, Mr. Song?"

"I was just thinking about my son. You remind me of Davy. You were both very good pianists. Nicholas, do you truly enjoy playing the piano?"

"Yes."

"That's good. Don't you ever leave your mother's side. You're all she has."

As the days went by, Johann sensed that something was not quite right with Nicole. One afternoon, after playing a set of her CDs that included Pink Floyd and Nirvana, Nicole began crying.

"What's wrong?" said Johann.

"Sometimes, I think you only want me for one thing," she said.

"Nicole."

"Let me finish. As soon as I take Nicholas to school, we do it. We do it in the morning. We do it at night. Sometimes we even do it during lunch breaks. I mean, I don't think this is the way to conduct a healthy relationship. You can't base a relationship on only one thing."

"Nicole, that's not true."

"Yes, it is. You only want me for my CD collection."

Johann uncovered the Ziploc bag with the bloody scissors that had claimed his son's life. As he held the red-handled scissors in his hand, he decided to tell Nicole and Nicholas the truth behind Davy's premature death.

"I have something to tell you," said Johann, that night.

"I have something to tell you, too," said Nicole.

"You first."

"I'm leaving for New York. I think the move will be good for Nicholas. He could improve his piano skills there. And who knows? Maybe I can find a gig or two in the Big Apple myself."

"Is that what he really wants?"

"Yes."

"And what about us?"

"Us? You'll do fine without Nicholas and me. That's the sense I get from you. You lose things but find them again. One door closes, another opens. That kind of thing. Now what were you gonna tell me?"

"Never mind."

So Nicole and Nicholas left. Nicholas gave Johann a CD of Bach's Art of the Fugue, the same music he had brilliantly performed during their first meeting at Orvis Auditorium.

"I know you probably own a hundred copies of this," wrote Nicholas, on a yellow post-it note. "But this is my favorite and I want you to have it. Maybe every time you play it, you can think of your mom and me."

As Johann held the gift up to the light, he realized something. All too quickly, his world had collapsed. Again. One day, he had been blessed with Joy and Davy. But they were taken from him. Then came Nicole and Nicholas. Now, he'd lost them, too.

At work, as Johann played Mahler and Bizet, he watched nervously as mainland corporate bigwigs sauntered through the radio station, looking unimpressed. At home, Johann longed to hear Nicole—once again—delineate the intricacies of Boston's early work, discuss AC/DC's guitar stylings, interpret the lyrics of Kansas' Dust in the Wind.

And he longed to hear young Nicholas sigh, roll his eyes to the ceiling and say, "Rock is just another four-letter word."

Johann stayed away from the next Hawaii Radio Broadcasters Awards Dinner. Instead, he spent the one-year anniversary of his meeting with Nicole at home, staring at the empty chairs and sofas she and her gifted son—for too brief a time—once occupied. He picked up a newspaper, turned to the ad that read 1-888-HOT BODY, and dialed the telephone. After a while, he was connected to someone named Maxine the Hollywood Aerobics Instructor.

"Hi, Handsome," Maxine purred. "You caught me right in the middle of my workout. I'm doing squats now. It's so hooooot. I'm just sweating. Mmmmm. Maybe I should take off my leotard. Would you like that?"

"Listen," said Johann. "I'm sorry. I'm trying to reach someone else. Is there a, um, Kimiko the Geisha there?"

"All right. Be that way. Why does everyone want Kimiko? Whatever. Have your credit card number ready and I'll connect you."

Johann listened anxiously as the telephone rang again.

"Hello?" said the woman on the other end of the phone. "Moshi-moshi. I've been waiting for your call."

Indian Summer

alexis rhone fancher

Sunday nights we'd drag the double mattress
to the roof, sleep under the stars, naked,
on cool, silk sheets that caught the moonlight.
I dazzled the heavens, my breasts fluorescent,
pin point nipples saluting the galaxies.

Your cock, darker than the rest of you,
would slip between my thighs.

You were better than any drug.

Friday and Saturday nights we'd head for North Beach
in our thrift shop finery (my see-through
dress and platform shoes, your big black boots);
after-hours at Keystone Korners, you'd sit in with Freddy
Hubbard or Elvin Jones, play keyboards while I
listened from my ringside table.

I knew you'd be famous. Your name
on the club's marquee, a recording contract
just a kiss away.

Meanwhile, you trawled the musicians' union
for session work, paying gigs (weddings, bar mitzvahs), played
security guard at the Hofbrauhaus, coming home
at 3am, a purloined brisket or pork roast under your jacket,
cooked to perfection. Still warm.

Some nights, I'd sit at the bar, nursing a whisky,
watch you play adagios on the holster of your gun to combat
boredom, a scowl on your face, like you were straddling
the fence between guarding the place or robbing it,

each of us dreaming of Sunday nights when
we'd lie together on the rooftop, complicit
in the steamy heat, searching each other's
faces for some secret, lost between us,

like how we fell in love in the first place.

Boys Before

brittany ackerman

I.

You were named after our state fish. You were my first friend in Florida. You might have been the only person who ever understood me. I moved to Florida when I was eight, the summer before fourth grade. I had to interview to get into the private school. I wore a skirt whose pattern was made to look like piano keys. I folded my hands in my lap while the principal asked me questions. I remember you walking in after me. You were a cute boy: curly hair, thin, a little lanky, piercing brown eyes. We both hated school. You were bored, too intelligent. I was anxious, too aware.

You told me what head was. "It's when you take your head and do crazy, disgusting things with it." You weren't wrong. You and the girl who had my same name teased me for not knowing about sex. The two of you on the playground, hands over mouths, whispering about me while I climbed from bar-to-bar, calloused my palms, trying to be good at something, at least.

I begged my mom to buy me a makeup kit from Limited Too. It was twenty-five dollars. It came with eyeshadow, blush, lipstick, a mirror. I put on blue eyeshadow and purple lipstick and came to school in a leopard sweater, the one with the black heart in the middle of the chest. I got out of my mom's car, walked up the stairs. It was the last day of fourth grade. There was a party in the room. You were at the computer in the corner playing a game. You turned around and laughed when you saw me. Everyone knew I loved you then.

You had a friend who used to prank call me. I was so scared of him when I was nine, ten, eleven. The calls came and went, came and went. He knew what to say to terrify me, the things he wanted to do. I never knew what he looked like. I only knew his name until I saw him post on your wall that you were gone. I clicked on his face, a bald-headed man with a buff body. He had the same name as a poet we studied in school, the one with the lame foot, and I had to write a report on him, the poet. I felt sick to my stomach researching that name over and over again. The fact that there was a Lord in front of it made things worse, a forced worship, a required admiration.

My mom made me go to day-camp one year at Pine Crest. I hated the girls in my "cabin," an empty school classroom we changed in for swim and otherwise spent no time in. There was Brett, a girl in my group who had a flat head and was popular. The camp made us pick names for our bunks, something space-themed that summer, and no one cared. No one volunteered a single thing. "Lunar Ladies," I suggested, a last-ditch effort to make friends. The counselor, a teenager who wore the camp's staff shirt tied up to show her stomach with tiny jean shorts, picked me up and twirled me like that scene in *Dirty Dancing*. No one respected me after that. I saw you in the cafeteria and thought you must have been a mirage. I ran and hugged you at your lunch table. "Brett is in your cabin?" you asked, disgusted. "Stay away from her," you warned. We only saw each other from across the camp or when traversing activities. We'd make obscene gestures as we passed one another, you hanging yourself with an imaginary noose at the kickball field, me shooting myself in the head at arts and crafts. I always had trouble making friends. I still do. I sit here now, remembering the way you told me at the end of the summer you were switching schools, that you'd write. You didn't say you'd miss me, but I knew you would. Brett told me the two of you had kissed the previous summer. She told me because she knew how I felt even though I tried so hard not to show it. She told me in a way that made it sound like I could have you then, like she was done, had her turn, and was passing you onto me.

You were my partner for a science project. You said to come to your house, that your mom would get us McDonald's. I can't remember her face at all. I know she had long, black hair. I know she wore sunglasses inside and moved slow. "Don't forget my goddamn apple pie!" You screamed at her, a joke she knew was a joke. She left us alone and you told me to take my shoes off by your bed. I kept thinking you were going to kiss me. Your older brother was away at a math competition. My brother was always away at math competitions too. Just us in that room. It took thirty-five minutes to get to your house. You picked up my shoes and smelled the inside. "Your feet don't even smell!"

In fourth grade you chased me up the stairs to our classroom and I fell. I scraped my elbow so bad I couldn't bend it for a week. Our teacher asked what happened and I told her I fell, but not that you chased me. I didn't want you to get in trouble. I was so upset though. I bled on my school uniform shirt. You just laughed. Now I know the laughter was out of shock, the surprise of hurting someone. I never told on you, all those times you hurt me. Instead, I keep a picture of us in front of Dave and Buster's wearing balloon hats the dinner magician made us. Instead, I think of your mother, her long fingers smelling of smoke, her love for you, her youngest son.

You write. You send me a small blue rock in the mail. You say it's an invincible rock, to go ahead, try it, slam the rock on any surface, drop it from the roof; it won't crack. I never try. I see your face when I hold the rock in my hand. I can see the rock now, even though it's gone. It is Prussian blue with grey rings at the top. It's shaped like Florida, but more scrunched together, the top wider, the bottom sort of dropping off. You ask if I've been watching *Malcolm in the Middle*. It's your favorite show. I will never be this close to you again. At your funeral, guests were asked to wear white or colors. It was a celebration of life.

II.

I met you in the Bahamas in line for the slide, the one that goes underwater through the shark tank. Kids waited up to an hour to ride. I was twelve. You were twelve. We were both on vacation with our families. On the first night I walked around the property with my family admiring the fish in large tanks, the vast casino that took up two whole buildings, the beautiful beach. I felt a pang in my chest, a longing for love. Every vacation was a chance at this love. My family was an obstacle, the thing I had to get around in order to succeed.

The next day, I saw you in line. You were with another boy, someone chubby. You were thin. You had boyish muscles, blonde hair, blue eyes. "Hi, I'm Shane," you said, and I introduced myself too like my dad taught me, reaching out my hand to shake yours. It felt like a miracle, you wanting to know me. You laughed. We hung out all day, an unspoken bond that started with me proving myself fearless as I rode down the big slide. You hugged me, our wet kid bodies together. I felt my bathing suit cling to my flat chest.

We ran up and down the stairs holding inner tubes. We rode all the slides that day, hundreds of times. My mom was looking for me. She told me we had dinner reservations and I had to go shower and get dressed. We said goodbye and see you tomorrow and all night I spoke of you, how wonderful you were. "So happy you made a friend," my mom said, but she didn't know it was more, she didn't realize.

I asked if I could walk around, enjoy the night air, but really I wanted to see if you were in the hotel movie theater or hanging out anywhere. She said I had to be back in the room in an hour. I walked the property like I had done the night before with my family. I was worried I might see my brother coming back from the game room or my dad venturing off to the casino. Worse, I worried my mom might spy on me like she did sometimes. But I didn't find you anywhere. I walked through the underground tanks and saw schools of exotic fish fluttering across my eye line. It was the kind of thing that would be beautiful if you had a lover.

The next few days were spent in a deep depression, the kind of sulking you're supposed to get good at in college. I forfeited Scrabble games with my mom, unable to find the words amongst my letters. I slept late and missed breakfast every day; I only ate chips and salsa from the pool bar. I asked to be excused from dinner so I could step deep into the hotel's belly, look around for you, go back to my seat at the table and sulk more. It was the first time I had ever wanted someone so bad and not something. When I was six, I stole a Barbie dress from KB Toys because I couldn't leave the store without it. It was a shiny, silver dress, futuristic looking, and I imagined my Barbie wearing it, coming from the future to visit Ken, tell him of their relationship he was unaware of, like in the movies. At first, he wouldn't believe her, but after they spent some time together, dinner and a kiss, he'd fall in love, just like he was supposed to. I palmed the dress from the dollar bin, my little hands sweaty with nervous energy, and made it out of the store without setting off the alarm. But once I opened my hand and revealed the dress my mom saw and made me go back inside and apologize. The thing is, I stole again after that, time-and-time again. I thought I deserved to get what I wanted, even if it was wrong.

On the last day of our trip, someone famous was at the pool bar having lunch. There was a crowd, cameras, commotion. My mom dragged me over to try and see who it was and I saw you out of the corner of my eye. My world stopped. I didn't know what to do. The words "play it cool" entered my mind like a message from God, so I stood there, feigning interest in the celebrity, covering my eyes with my hand to block the sun.

"Hey!" you called out. I stood still, pretending not to hear. You ran over, tapped me on the shoulder. "Wanna go on the slide?" you asked. I departed from my mom and we got in line for the big slide. The slide was called The Leap of Faith and until then, I had only associated those words with my dad's favorite Indiana Jones movie where Indy has to take a leap of faith and spell the name of God with the letters on the ground in order to save his dad. "Only the penitent man will pass," my dad's favorite line. I never knew what that word meant, but in my own understanding I took it to mean important because it sounded similar, but really it means remorseful or apologetic. I wouldn't learn about that kind of stuff until much later, but the phrase stuck in my mind as we climbed the stairs that day. I wanted to say something like, "Hey, Shane, am I *penitent* to you?" and have you be impressed at my vocabulary. But then when we got to the top of the line you held my hand, like no one before had ever done. I'd only held hands with my mom or other kids at school when I was little, never in a romantic way. You held it for some time, and let go only to descend the 60-foot body slide and speed through the glass tunnel surrounded by a shark-filled lagoon. I was still smiling by the time the lifeguard told me I was clear to go down, too.

When it got dark, you asked the woman at the temporary tattoo and hair braiding stand for a piece of paper and a pen. The teal *Atlantis*, Bahamas pen shook in my hand as I wrote down my full name, address, phone number. "Florida," you said, "I've got an Aunt out there. Maybe I could come visit!" You sounded so happy, like a kid in a holiday commercial who got all the Christmas presents he wanted.

You said you lived in Texas but weren't specific about which part. Texas sounded far away. And it was. I'd never been there before, but imagined a vast desert, tumbleweed, cacti, sand, lots of sand.

A few weeks later you called from Texas. You told me I was so pretty, you could have kissed me at the slide that day. I asked for your email address so I could write you a letter. "I like getting emails," you said, sounding hopeful. I cried when we hung up. I remembered your lips and they had looked quite nice. You only called the one time. I never found your profile online or anything like that. I didn't even know your last name. When I used to search *Shane, blonde, Texas,* there were too many faces to sort though, too many people that could have very well been you or not have been you at all.

I sent an email to the address you gave me on the phone. I didn't hesitate to write because this was love, I thought. This kind of thing surpassed all else, the normal order of the world. I told you I thought we were perfect for each other, that I'd love to come and visit you someday, or that you could come stay with me when you visited your Aunt. I told you I'd wanted to find love on that trip and that I had, and that it felt so good. I told you about the pang in my chest. You never wrote back.

That was the year we read *Romeo and Juliet* in school and something happened to me. I started to think differently. Forbidden love, unrequited love, unfaltering, unwavering love: all of it consumed me. Some days, I wore my hair in pigtails. I started rolling my uniform skirt up three inches past my knees.

III.

I was in love with a boy named David when I was fourteen. I suppose he was my first obsession. There have been many since. A quick Google search shows he is now a sort of mobster living in Miami. His last post was a picture of a case of AR15 assault rifles with the hashtag #*toys*.

I was riding my bike around my neighborhood after school, still in my uniform, when I saw two boys walking home. They were in their uniforms too. One of them called out to me. I slowed down, came to a stop, hopped off my bike, curious. He said his name was Mike and he had his polo shirt tucked into his khaki pants. The other boy was David, and he didn't say anything that afternoon. I don't think we actually spoke all that much ever, but in my mind it was romantic, what had happened.

I agreed to come to Mike's house after my parents went to dinner. A sneak-out. I rode my bike one subdivision over and found his house. I knocked on the door and he answered. "You could have rang the bell," he said. He was still in his polo shirt but wearing basketball shorts now instead of his pleated pants. I wondered if David was still there, if that was part of the deal.

Mike took me upstairs to his room. I remember his comforter was burgundy. There were Red Hot Chili Peppers posters everywhere, CD inserts taken out and held to the wall with poster putty. Mike walked over to his computer chair and started playing music. David came out of the bathroom and laid down on the bed. "I'll be right back," Mike said and ran out of the room. I was still standing in the doorway.

"Come here," David said, and I kicked off my sneakers, climbed onto the bed and sat next to him. David pulled me on top of him and kissed me. He pulled away, then smiled and kissed me again but with tongue. "You're a pretty girl, you know that?" He said and I shook my head no. Mike came back in the room holding an unlabeled bottle. David sat up. Mike explained it was liquor, stuff he had mixed together from a few different bottles downstairs. He took a big sip and we all took turns until it was gone. I had to walk my bike home when it was time to leave.

I never got David's number, so the only way to David was through Mike. But I think Mike was jealous or something, and he wouldn't let me see him. But one night Mike called and told me to come over. He said David was there and wanted to see me. I couldn't get ready fast enough and ended up putting on too much eyeliner.

When I rode up to the house, I saw a few other bikes in the driveway. I rang the doorbell and a boy wearing only a pair of basketball shorts answered the door. He smiled and opened the door wide enough for me to come in. "Where's Mike?" I asked and he laughed. Then Mike came running downstairs and seemed out of breath. "See, I told you guys I'd get her here."

Joel and Brett were the boys I had never met before. They both had bleached hair and spiked tips. The boys circled around me and shoved each other around. "Who wants her?" Brett asked "Mike?" I said, confused and worried. "They're just being dicks," Mike said. "Where's David?" I asked. All the boys laughed. "Listen," said Joel, "We know you *love* David, but I don't think that's gonna work out." I froze. "Do you want to go swimming?" he asked. "I don't have a bathing suit," I said. "That's okay," he laughed, they all laughed. I was wearing a black push-up bra I got from Victoria's Secret and a matching thong. I had never been in my underwear in front of a boy before, but I felt like I had to prove myself. Maybe if these boys liked me, David would like me back.

I took off my shirt and balled it tight in my hand. I stood there waiting for what was next. A part of me still thought maybe David was upstairs, that he would come down and save me.

Joel grabbed my arm and took me outside to the pool. I looked at the water; it was the bluest thing I'd ever seen, turquois and glowing in Mike's expensive outdoor lighting of the Woodfield Country Club we both lived in. I was cold and scared and it was clear the rest of my life would be like this, things I didn't want to do but had to in order to prove myself. I wanted to go home. Joel kissed me and shoved his tongue down my throat. It was horrible, nothing like David's sweet kiss. Joel touched my chest and asked me to take off my bra. I turned around to leave. "You're a prude," Joel said. "David was right."

Joel became a lawyer. His photo online is outlined in blue. His latest post, how to incorporate Saturday morning work hours into your workweek, "Not only will you feel good about it, but watch your results elevate." Brett is nowhere to be found online, but we shared a kiss at a party years later and he was nice to me. Mike moved across the globe and I never told him how much I was hurt by that ambush. I guess I understood the need to be popular, but it came at a cost. Maybe I had to pay because everything I loved was right in front of me.

poem

The Licensed Freedom of Marital Sex
—for Tim. himself

jo-anne cappeluti

It's animal passion licensed to be
free (behind closed doors) to shake and snort
beg and whine for toothsome scraps and show its thanks by
licking unabashedly whatever's at hand.

Even outside, unmuzzled, it's leashed
free to turn its head now and then to various scents
and shapes passing by
because you know
it will never be in any need

of a choke chain—

That's Nick Bottom

jason wallace

I am a high school special education teacher. This means I deal with our school's mentally and emotionally crippled, the hyperactive, the distracted, the disturbed. And this is before I make my way out of the staff lounge. Thank God I have the kids to turn to.

I never set out to be a special-ed teacher. I had big dreams coming out of college. I was going to be an attorney in San Francisco or maybe a CPA in Los Angeles. I even dreamed of combining the two and becoming an agent in Hollywood. I was going to marry a trophy wife and drive an Aston Martin. Sip spritzers from my Monticeto veranda and watch the sun set behind the Pacific. Instead, I went to a state college, got a degree in English, worked as a manager of a Denny's until I couldn't take it anymore, and then when the state of California was hard up for teachers, I got an emergency credential and jumped ship. I figured I'd teach English in some quaint suburban high school, parsing sentences and acting out Shakespeare, maybe show a movie every couple of weeks.

"High school English teachers are a dime a dozen," the principal said. My interview was about to take a turn.

"Okay. Maybe I could teach history?" I asked.

"Actually, have you ever thought about teaching special ed?"

"Um, not really." I had a vision of students banging their heads against the walls while others smoked cigarettes at their desks and threw paper airplanes at me.

"Well, we need a special ed teacher. You're a big guy. The kids will respect you." The principal presented this bit of information as if it was an ultimatum wrapped up in a sales pitch.

"I guess I could give it a try."

"Attaboy."

"This will only be for a year, right? Just to get my foot in the door?"

"Of course. Just for a year," the principal said. He stood to shake my hand as if we had just closed a deal on beachfront property in Nebraska.

That was fifteen years ago.

The job has its perks. There isn't a lot expected of my kids, so there isn't a lot that's expected of me. If I were a lazy teacher, I could simply hand out worksheets to keep the kids busy, bribe them with candy and promises of "chill time," and show movies every other day. Anything to keep the kids occupied, especially when the administrators pop in, which they rarely do, unless one of my students blows up a toilet with an M-80 or beats someone up or cusses out a hall monitor.

The first time I walked into my resource junior English class, I realized those kids had a deep hunger for two things: attention and the desire to actually learn something.

"So, you're the new teacher," a kid named Dave said. He looked normal. A little unkempt and squirrely, but no different from any other sixteen-year-old boy who spent his waking hours outside of school riding a BMX bike or skateboard.

"Yep. That's me."

"The last teacher was hauled off in a police car," a girl named Lois said. She had big eyes and uneven bangs. She looked like someone who smoked cigarettes.

"I miss Mrs. Lee," said Arnie. He had autism. I knew this because when he introduced himself to me before the class started, he said, "My name is Arnie and I am autistic. Are you autistic?" I told him that I wasn't, that I was an English teacher.

"Why was Mrs. Lee hauled off in a police car?" I asked.

"Because she was a crazy bitch," Dave said. Kids snickered. Arnie looked quickly at Dave, then me, unsure of whether or not he was supposed to snicker too.

"All Mrs. Lee did was show movies. We saw *The Little Mermaid* sixteen times," someone said, trying to ease the tension.

"Let's watch the language," I said. I looked straight at Dave and used my serious voice. I even puffed my chest out a bit. I figured I needed to put Dave in his place quickly, before things got out of hand. He was clearly the leader. The others would follow. Arnie jammed his fingers in his ears and began muttering to himself.

"Oh, okay Mr. Man," Dave said. "Just promise you won't beat me up." A couple of the boys laughed. The rest of the class was silent. They waited to see who'd flinch first. I liked Dave. He reminded me of myself at sixteen. Except I didn't have the balls to talk back to a teacher. Dave was about to become the teacher's pet.

"Dave," I said. "This is gonna be a great year. Now shut up before I squish your fucking guts out." The class got so quiet you could hear a weed trimmer whirring on the other side of the campus. I didn't care if I got fired. I wanted to be a regular English teacher anyway.

"Cool," he said. He was grinning. I had him. I had all of them. Thank God there were no administrators around.

I spent that first year teaching the hell out of the subject. I taught my students about nouns and verbs and adjectives. I taught them about participles even though I wasn't sure what one was. It was in the book though. I taught them the FANBOYS, how to write simple and compound sentences, how to write business letters, haiku, flash fiction, three-paragraph essays, five-paragraph essays, and research papers. "Research papers?" they screamed. "We want to watch *The Little Mermaid*," they pleaded. The only movie I let them watch was *Dead Poet's Society*. Only once. Just before the winter break. A little Christmas present from me.

In the fall we read *Hamlet*. In the spring we read *A Midsummer Night's Dream*. "Oh, this is the play in the movie," they said. I told them I was thrilled they made the connection and for a reward I assigned them an Updike short story: "Tomorrow and Tomorrow and So Forth." And the kids soaked all the information up. Not like sponges. "Like thirsty drunks bathing in a pool of whiskey." That was one of Dave's stabs at metaphor. They processed the information in their various ways: some quicker than others, some in unique and bizarre ways. A few just didn't get it. Not unlike any other high school English class.

Of course, not everything went smoothly. Kids had their good days and bad. There were fights, one kid shit her pants, and I got cussed out at least once every two weeks. And as much as I liked Dave, he seemed to fight awfully hard with the process of learning. He was happy to run errands to the office and escort Jenny, who had cerebral palsy, from class to class. He was a gentleman that way. But when I would ask him a question, he'd either play dumb or offer some smartass response. Sometimes the responses were clever. Mostly they were annoying. A few times I let him run an errand only to have him hauled in by a vice principal for smoking in the bathroom. He didn't have enough money to vape. He stole the cigarettes from his mom or bummed them off bums. The VP asked me later why I trusted Dave. I didn't have a good answer.

Things weren't going well for Dave at home. His mother was a meth head and "boyfriends" came and went as they pleased. One Friday morning he walked in with dark bags under his eyes, as if he'd been up for two days. It was twenty minutes before lunch, and I was on my prep. I had the room to myself and was listening to Iron and Wine on Youtube. Dave's hoodie had twigs and leaves stuck to it. He smelled of BO and wood smoke. I hadn't seen him since Tuesday.

"Where the hell have you been?" I asked.

"I been sleeping at the river since Tuesday."

"You mean *by* the river."

"Fuckin' whatever," he said. He was in no mood for grammar. He plopped into a desk. His shoes were caked in mud.

"Have you eaten?"

"I had a few Starbursts yesterday."

"C'mon, let's go out to my car."

I pulled my lunchbox from the backseat. I stopped keeping my lunch in the staff lounge fridge. Teachers would help themselves to my chips and fruit cups. No one tells you that in teacher education classes.

"Here, eat it all. "

"Thanks. Hey Mr. H, you got a smoke?" I gave him one of my Camels. He pushed in the car's lighter. It popped out and he lit his cigarette. Him smoking in my car probably could've gotten me fired. A letter in my file at the least. But he seemed to really need a smoke at that moment. Plus, my car was parked in a secluded part of the faculty parking lot out by the dumpster. No one except me parked there. The bell for lunch rang. We could see kids spilling into the hallways, like ants pouring from their holes.

"You ever noticed how the coils in a car's lighter look like tiny tree rings?" Dave asked.

"Where are you sleeping tonight, Dave?"

"Same place. I ain't going home."

"I've got to call CPS. You know that, right? Maybe they can hook you up with a safe, clean place tonight."

"Go ahead and call, but I'm going to the river. I like it there."

He had a good point. It was pretty and the late spring air had been warm. He wasn't going to freeze and most of the vagrants stayed closer to the city. There were worse places. I wasn't going to invite him home with me. Not that I thought it weird or anything. I just didn't want to start fostering kids. There were too many to take care of, like stray dogs and cats.

"Does the river go out to the ocean?" Dave asked. He had a mouthful of bologna sandwich. I asked for a hit from his smoke. He passed it to me, and I took a long drag and handed it back.

"It does. But first it flows past Stockton."

"It's kinda like life then," he said, "going through a shitty part before it can reach something good."

"Yeah, it kind of is."

We shared a second cigarette. The bell to end lunch rang.

"Well, it's time to get back. Time to wake up from our enchanted slumber," I said. I get whimsical after I've had a smoke.

We made our way through the B-wing hallway. I was thinking about the CPS report I'd have to write up. I also needed to contact a counselor to see if there was some kind of support service our district could offer a kid like Dave. Something besides a free school lunch. We passed Mr. Mularkey's room. He taught AP English and on the outer wall of his room, a former student had painted a mural of Nick Bottom chasing Puck. The Puck looked like Peter Pan and Bottom looked like, well, a donkey.

"Hey, that's Nick Bottom." Dave said. "How come they didn't paint a human body?"

I stopped and smiled. I assumed Dave slept through or didn't pay attention to my *Midsummer Night's* lectures. I was kind of shocked, but pleased.

"You know that's Bottom?"

"Why the fuck wouldn't I? You sure talk about him enough."

"So you assholes actually listen to me?"

"It's not like we have anything else to do."

I pat Dave on the back and gave his neck a firm squeeze. I couldn't help it. I was really liking him at that moment. And I always felt happy after a smoke. Dave didn't flinch or pull away. He trusted me. He probably needed an adult like me. My only hope was that I was up to the challenge.

Sonnet Spooning

andrena zawinski

I taught my love to spoon, not in bed, thigh
to thigh up against each other, no feet
layered one upon the other, no arm
ribboning belly, but with tablespoons,
Allons Danser on the radio, two
spoons pulled from their huddle in a drawer
to bang against each other, held real loose,
ends balanced between thumb and forefinger.

I taught my love to slap the thigh and palm
to make spoons bounce and click and clang and clap
in an idiophonic percussion
of Cajun sound beyond scooping gumbo.
Next we will work the steel washboard rhythm
with pop can rings. Allons danser. Let's spoon.

The Yosemite Bear Bandits

frank scozzari

The silence of the midnight valley was broken by the patter of running feet.

Then came the cry—"Bear!"

And again, a different voice. "Bear! Bear!"

And then a chorus of: "Bears!"

Lantern lights came on, flashlight beams cut through the darkness, and my two buddies came shuffling past me, grinning.

"Teatime," Rob said.

He was on one end of an ice chest and George on the other, each holding a handle, moving awkwardly. I watched them disappear into the dark forest behind me. Then I turned my attention back to the campsites, where the door of a nearby camper opened. A man dressed in long johns poked his head out and glared into the darkness. He came out and walked in my direction, carrying a lantern in one hand and a hammer in the other. He looked like he wanted to tangle but stopped at the edge of the forest.

"They took my chest!" he yelled. "Goddamned bears took my ice chest!"

Neighboring campers emerged from all different directions, gathering at his campsite. There was a little boy holding a brownie camera with a flash on top. Another little boy held a toy tomahawk with his parents standing guard beside him.

"It was sitting right there," the man explained, pointing. "It was sitting right there on the table. Goddamned bears carried it off!"

"I'll be damned," one camper said, shaking his head.

Flashlight beams searched the forest beyond the lantern light while I ducked low behind a large Douglas fir, snickering. None of the campers were brave enough to venture too far, and even if they did, I would just pop my head out and claim to have come from the next campground upriver. Instead, they stood there, all bewildered, like a herd of wildebeests looking at the carcass of a fallen comrade.

Dumbasses, I thought.

I watched for several entertaining minutes before I turned and followed my companions along the dark trail back to Happy Isles.

It was the summer of '73 and the Hippies were in Yosemite in full force. They were there to celebrate living and nature and the human spirit and the hope for world peace. That high-tide mark that Hunter Thompson talked about hadn't crested yet and beautiful spirits roamed freely, sometimes nakedly, through the meadows and along the Merced. They held nightly love-ins at Happy Isles and you could hear the music echoing all the way down the Valley. And if you looked up at Glacier Point, you could see the shadows of celestial dancers stretching high on the granite walls. Bead-laden sun worshippers lay out on the granite boulders along the river. Hippie goddesses bathed naked beneath the waterfalls. Guitar strumming and flute playing troubadours strolled the Park's roadways. I think I even saw Joni Mitchell's child of God walking along the road with a bong strapped to his back.

Everywhere you went there was bliss, except for the ranger stations. The rangers were crew-cut, red-necked Korean War vets looking to smash some free-spirited heads. There had been an incident in a meadow where baton-wielding rangers stormed a love-in on horseback. Many Hippies were hospitalized, but it only made them more resolute, more anti-government and more anarchical.

That was the Yosemite we stumbled into, four trail-worn kids looking for food, essentially anything that was edible. We had been hiking the John Muir Trail, a two-hundred-and-ten mile trek through pure wilderness along the backbone of the High Sierra, traversing snow-covered passes, fording raging rivers, warming freezing feet by campfire, and surviving off dehydrated food cooked by butane stove. When we reached our food stash at Florence Lake and found the marmots had gotten into it and eaten half of it, we had to improvise. And improvise we did, very well. We became mountain marauders, wild misfits who could even compete with the raccoons and bears for food.

When we first arrived in Yosemite Valley, we relied on the Hippies. They welcomed everyone in communal fashion. Into a huge pot, everyone added something—a can of Campbell's tomato soup, a can Dennison's chili beans, Spaghetti-Os, chicken broth—and anyone with a sierra cup or an empty can or a somewhat clean hand could dip into the pot and pull out dinner. We had made our camp only a short distance upriver from Happy Isles—a cave-like hideaway along the Merced beneath a large granite overhang—which made this arrangement with the Hippies very convenient. We partook several times, contributing nothing, yet dipping our Sierra cups into the Hippie-stew, often multiple times. And they were liberal with their alcoholic spirits as well. Pull an empty gallon jug from a trash can and go from one hippy campsite to the next, finding half a beer here, some wine there, the last drops from a whisky bottle, a little rum, or whatever, and four teenagers had enough brew to get an army drunk.

Each evening of our first several days in the Valley, we'd return to our cave, full-bellied, and we'd sip and lay flat, and fat, in the pine needles. But as usual, when things were going good, we became discontent. We got bored. The Hippie soup concoction got old. We craved something better, and as boys do, we planned and devised and schemed. It became our daily routine to scour campsites for unattended ice chests, and our nightly routine to commandeer them. The way we saw it, we were providing a service to the weekend adventurers, all those L.A. urban dwellers who ventured into the wilderness only one week per year. We bestowed upon them a once-in-a-lifetime-into-the-wild experience, the telling of which could be passed down through the generations.

We weren't bad kids, we convinced ourselves. We were just hungry.

The rangers, of course, knew bears didn't carry off ice chests—bears simply demolished them on the spot. So they sought out us human bears. The evidence of our labor piled high beneath the overhanging rock we called home in the form of a pyramid of ice chests, stacked six high. On top was our prize: a red, white, and blue stars-and-stripes, lacquered-finished, custom Coleman.

Now we examined the bounty of our nightly catch and found the pickings to be slim. The ice chest contained only half a package of Oscar Myer hot dogs, five to be exact, mustard, no buns but a quarter loaf of bread, three cans of coke, and a ton of ice.

"Looks like they were ready to leave."

"Why all the ice?"

"Maybe we need to be more picky."

Willie, the youngest among us, had stayed back at the camp and had a fire going when we arrived. He had made it correctly this time, keeping the flames low beneath the encircling-boulders so they could not be seen from the trail above or the road down at Happy Isles. Rob proportioned our catch evenly. The morsels looked pitiful. One-and-a-quarter hotdogs each, one-and-a-half slices of bread each, and a few ounces of coke poured into our Sierra cups. We stuck our dogs on sticks and cooked them. Then we stuck them in between a slice of bread, added tons of mustard, and washed them down with the divvied-up coke. After we were through, George carried the empty chest to the back of the den and stacked it with the others.

Silence prevailed as the campfire burned down. The glowing embers lit our hungry faces. Somebody's stomach growled.

"It's hit or miss," George finally said.

"We need to be more particular," said Rob.

"We need to stick with the best tents or the Winnebago's," I said. "If they have a luxury tent and good equipment, then they'll have good food."

"That's what I mean," Rob said, and he stuck his stick in the fire and moved the coals around. "I don't want to eat that Hippy shit anymore."

"Me neither," said George.

Rob looked around at our glowing faces. "I want more steak."

We had gotten steak in one of the stolen ice chests, and it was our best feast yet.

"Hamburger will do," George said.

"I saw a campsite with a Cadillac and an Airstream yesterday," Willie said.

"Where?" I asked.

"Upper Pines—I think."

"Was it Upper Pines or not?"

"I think so. We passed it on the bus."

"Okay, we'll ride the bus again tomorrow. We'll take a double-decker and stake out the best campsites."

"Yeah," Willie said, "and maybe I'll find that Cadillac again."

"We'll look for campsites with multiple tents, good tents."

"And a lot of children," said George. "Children need food."

"And parents usually have beer or wine," I said.

I looked over at Rob, who was shaking his head as he stirred the coals with his stick.

"What'ya thinking?"

"We've hunted and scavenged and begged," he said. "We've gotten lucky sometimes, and sometimes we haven't."

"Yeah."

"We've eaten Hippy shit."

"Yeah, what's your point?"

"Why scavenge when we have a shit-load of food right here at our feet?"

George and Willie exchanged glances.

I just looked at Rob, bewildered.

"The snack bar, Dummies."

He was referring to the concession stand at Happy Isles, which was open during the day and boarded up at night. It was loaded with all the kinds of junk food teenagers love.

No one said anything. We were all aware of the snack stand. We passed it every day on our way into the Village and had watched, covetously, as tourists purchased and ate hot dogs and ice-cream bars and drank Dr. Pepper and Crush. We had never considered busting into it. Breaking the law stealing ice chests was one thing; breaking into the snack stand would be felony larceny.

Rob slowly glanced around the campfire, stopping on my face. With the end of his stick he flicked little a coal in my direction. "Well?"

"There is food there," I said, matter-of-fact.

"They've got hamburgers," said George.

"And ice cream," said Willie.

"And they have cigarettes," said Rob. He was the only smoker.

I think we all thought of the Snickers bars, boxes of them.

"When?" I asked.

"Now," said Rob.

"Yeah, now," George nodded. "All the rangers have gone to bed and there're no Hippies tonight." He paused. "And I'm still hungry."

"So am I," said Rob.

I thought about it. It was past midnight. Happy Isles was the ghost town it should've been. And there were no Hippy music festivals going on.

"I could cut the cable with my axe," Rob said.

We all knew what he was talking about. The stand was secured each night with plywood boards secured by a cable-wrap, which could be cut with a sharp axe.

"You think you can cut that cable?"

Rob stared at me. Then he got up, went to his pack, took out his axe, and came back to the campfire. He took his seat and ran his finger over the blade. When he was being mischievous, he could put on one of those shit-eating grins, the kind that only Jack Nicholson could make, and he did that now.

"Yep. I think I can cut it." He hacked the air twice for dramatic effect.

Willie grinned widely too. "Yeah, that should do it."

Rob chopped the air with another practice swing of the axe.

We assembled into a unit, heading down the dark trail together along the white-flashing Merced. There was starlight, but where the forest was thick it was nearly black. Only out in the river could we see white. We could hear various echoes down-Valley—a garbage truck slamming dumpsters and some shouting voices—but they were distant sounds, none of which were of any concern to us.

We took our positions, and Rob and George started on the snack stand.

From where I stood watching the road, I could hear the action but couldn't see it. The first chop of the axe had a muted sound, the second a little louder. The third echoed off the granite base of Glacier Point.

Then the chopping became a flurry and, reaching a crescendo, there was a pause before one last loud Bang!

Then nothing.

I was getting nervous. The plan was for someone to come get me once they'd cut the cable, but no one had. There were no lights on the road and the only light I could see was up high at Glacier Point.

Finally, I walked to the snack stand to see what was going on.

The snack bar, which was a four-sided building about fifteen-foot square with a back door and an open counter facing the river, emerged in the starlight. What I saw, or thought I saw, was the bar open for business, as I had seen it so many times in daylight. Behind the counter, where the plywood had been removed, stood an attendant wearing one of those center-creased white café caps with two pointed ends.

It was Rob.

"How can I help you?" he said, sporting the Jack Nicholson grin.

George was already inside, rummaging through boxes. I could see his backside bobbing up and down as he went through the inventory. Willie suddenly appeared in the back door, which was now open.

"Take those," George told him, and Willie grabbed some boxes George had set aside and carried them out.

Rob grabbed the point of his café hat and tossed it out the opening. "C'mon, get in here and help!"

I went in through the back door. Willie was walking away with what I now saw to be a case of ice cream sandwiches.

We didn't handle this very systematically. We were more like pirates pillaging, or rats in a cheese factory. We took whatever, and as much as

gold man review

we could. By the time we left, it looked like bears had been there, for real. Boxes tipped over, some ripped open, shelves disheveled and emptied, refrigerator items unwrapped, bitten into, and carelessly discarded. We even left the damn freezer door open. And I'm sure our fingerprints were all over the place. We really didn't think about that kind of thing, nor did we care.

Exiting the back door with arms filled, I saw Willie sitting there at the base of a pine tree in full-lotus position gorging on the ice-cream sandwiches. He had white ice cream all around his lips.

"Come on," I yelled at him.

He wiped his mouth, got up, picked up the boxes, and followed me. I let him go ahead.

As we walked back up the dark trail, Rob carried a stack, three boxes high. The box on top was a case of Salem cigarettes. He had jerky strips and pepperoni sticks stuffed in and hanging out of his back pockets. George was equally loaded. Being the biggest of us, he managed four boxes, the top one pressed up against the side of his face. He had to eyeball the trail through a sliver of space between boxes. Willie had two big boxes, but he was still munching on ice-cream sandwiches. I know this because I could hear him, and every once in a while, an empty wrapper would drop to the trail in front of me and I'd pick it up.

"Hey! Don't leave a trail!"

He'd look back at me and shrug, and then do it again.

We reached our cave-like hideout exhausted. We set all the boxes down and took inventory: hot dogs, hamburger patties, buns, cases of Snickers, Almond Joy, and Mounds, cookies, and even a box of ketchup in those small little packets. Rob's prize was the case of Salem cigarettes, and he took to smoking one right away.

Everyone had already eaten something, either back at the snack bar or on the way back to camp. But we ate more now. We ate as many ice-cream sandwiches as we could before they melted. What was left we set afloat downriver in a box. We ate raw dogs, pepperoni sticks, and Snickers. Willie was moaning all night and eventually threw up, which caused a chain reaction. I remember, at one point, three of us lined up along the riverbank.

The next day, ranger trucks were all over the place. They stretched police tape around the concession stand. Tourist and hikers stopped and gawked.

We spied on them from a distance but stayed at our camp for the next two days, keeping out of sight, sunbathing on the large boulders along the riverbank, barebacked with big bellies. We had no need to go anywhere. We had more food than we could eat. We utilized the ice chests to preserve the food and also rigged a line in the icy river, at the end of which was a huge plastic bag full of perishables, weighed down with some stones.

But truly, we had taken too much, and much of it spoiled in the heat of the summer valley.

On the third day, we all headed into the Village. We slipped by the Rangers' crime line, acting shocked to see the concession stand still closed and taped up. We spent the day lounging around the Village. At one point, I saw Rob sitting at the entrance to the Village Store selling half-priced cigarettes. Somehow he didn't get caught. We heard some word about the snack bar break-in at Happy Isles. Rumor had it, among the day-hikers anyhow, that bears had done it.

Yeah, right, we thought. Bears with axes.

The rangers, of course, knew better. But they could never catch us.

We spent our last day in the Valley riding around on top of one of those double-decker buses, sliding jerky strips to one another, trading Almond Joys for Mounds bars, enjoying the sunshine and the breeze. I remember looking at Willie's face, which had been gaunt after the long trail, and noticing it looking fuller. We went back to Happy Isles for our packs and left with some misgivings. This granite overhang, nevertheless, had been our home for several weeks. We set the red, white, and blue custom Coleman ice chest afloat downriver, hoping for its return to its true owner. All the other ice chests we left stacked beneath the overhang, figuring someday someone would find them.

The postscript to all of this is a sad one. The Hippies were blamed for the snack bar break-in. The baton-wielding Rangers banned them from Happy Isles. They could no longer hold music festivals there, or for that matter, anywhere in the Valley—the crackdown became park-wide. It's funny how the sins of one can fall upon another—maybe not so funny, but that's what happened. We knew of this before we left the Valley. I remember the last night we stayed at our camp there was no song or music echoing down the valley. Nor did we see the shadows of celestial dancers high on the granite walls. Nor, on that last bus ride, did we see tie-dyed t-shirts and long dresses celebrating out in the meadows. We had crashed that long beautiful wave Hunter Thompson had written about—maybe not for the rest of the country, but certainly for Yosemite Valley.

On reflection, I would say, we had gone pretty low, and we were not really starving.

As with the sixties and seventies, we faded, becoming responsible (and law-abiding) adults. The Chinese say, once you have climbed a mountain together you are friends for life. It is also true about hiking the John Muir Trail. We have remained friends and have logged many more trail miles together, albeit better prepared and with secure food stashes. The craziness of youth was gone, but not the memory of it, not entirely.

Still, I can see Rob lounging in the last seat on top of the double-decker, bare-backed as usual, smoking one of those stolen Salem cigarettes. He's grinning that crazy Jack Nicholson grin, like he's in on some joke the rest of the world doesn't know about. I can't see his eyes because he's wearing dark sunglasses, but when he notices me looking at him, his grin widens, his lips move slowly and he says one word, loudly, in a low tone:

"BEAR!"

Aidan and His Therapist

h. william taeusch

Much appreciated for her no-nonsense directive counseling, Sylvia Cohen, a sought-after psychotherapist in Santa Barbara, suffered from her recent breakup with Joshua, her boyfriend of two years. He wanted kids. She didn't. She already had one, who didn't like Joshua. Her Sam was a mood-swinging twelve-year-old, interested in fishing. Joshua, no dummy, before—or was it because—he became an ex-boyfriend, had taken Sylvia and Sam out on a boat-for-hire, trolling off the Channel Islands. That was Joshua. He did things for Sylvia, it seemed, only in order to get something from her. This time, Joshua remained in the back of the boat inhaling diesel fumes and vomiting over the side while Sylvia helped Sam pull in a respectable salmon. So she changed her status on Facebook to irrevocably unattached. Two weeks later, she couldn't get the lyrics of the oldie out of her head, "Every night I hope and pray a dream lover will come my way."

So when Aidan came for a second visit, a patient who looked like a young Daniel Day-Lewis with his black curls, it was no wonder she felt a tickle in her third chakra. He worked at Kinkos in the back office, had some friends mainly at work, no girlfriend, no boyfriend, lived alone in a condo overlooking the Channel Islands. Didn't use drugs, a little alcohol, some pot. And he cut his forearms, watched the blood well up in a series of crimson beads, and contemplated cutting again, deeper. It was a habit, he said, that had started in the past year after he flunked out of graduate school.

Later that week, among the junk mail that fell through the slot in her front door, she found a handwritten letter from Aidan:

Dear Sylvia Cohen, LCSW
    Licensed   *frequently.*
        Clinical   *of*
            Social   *I think*
                Worker, who
I thought about you after our visit when I wanted to cut myself again. And then I didn't. Why? I don't know though we talked about it. Sometimes my mind wandered when we talked. But my heart fills with warmth and positive feelings. For life. And for you. Your office is such a safe place. And you emanate such warmth and understanding. It's like nothing I've ever felt before. It reminds me of that poem by Auden about truth or love or something...
When it comes, will it come without warning
Just as I'm picking my nose?

Will it knock on my door in the morning,
Or tread in the bus on my toes?
        Don't be alarmed. I'm not a stalker. Not a nut. Well…not a nut who would
hurt others. It's me who's out of whack, but when I run on the beach, I think of
you. That helps immensely (both the running and the thinking).
        Okay, I looked it up in the ethical guidelines for therapists…no sex of course,
but they allow appropriate touching! Though they don't define what that may be.
        I look forward to next Tuesday.

                        Fondly, Aidan

    She felt no real threat. The letter amused her—a young guy infatuated
with her. What was not to like? His letter had humor, self-deprecation, and
even Auden. This had happened before with a male client or two. Aidan had
to be no more than thirty; she was thirty-six. Aware of her feelings—what
she was trained for—she knew how to handle it.
    During the next week, Sylvia saw her other patients, mostly errant teen-
agers, their hormones out of control, craving the attention offered by an
adult—an adult who listened to what they said. Joshua emailed and wanted
to be friends, maybe more. Wasn't going to happen. With some effort, she
didn't think about Aidan's letter, which was over the line by discussing the
line. Aidan had Joshua's big expressive eyes. She buried that thought. Life
moved too fast these days for her to take the time to shrink herself down.
    The following Tuesday, after some consideration, she chose the beige silk
shirt to wear under a cashmere cardigan, no earrings. She wiggled into a
black skirt that stopped above the knees but, after a quick glance in the
mirror, took it off and pulled out a longer pleated skirt that complement-
ed her figure. Modest, less alluring, acceptable. Nothing wrong with liking
attention. Heels only moderately high. And the jade ring that Sam's father
had given her. For a necklace, on a simple gold chain, a golden apple with a
small bite out, a reminder of Eve's sin and a gift from the retailer who sold
her a new computer.
    Aidan was her first patient of the day. Traffic was heavy on 101 North.
She'd left plenty of time, but the steering of her Toyota hatchback slowly
became mushy, and she pulled over to the right lane. Something was wrong.
Maybe a wheel was coming off. She exited the freeway and popped open
her door, causing a motorcycle to swerve. The leathered rider gave her the
finger. Rattled, Sylvia went around on the gravel berm where she saw the
rear tire was flat. She pulled her cell phone from her purse and fished out
her Triple-A card. Though she reached a dispatcher immediately, it would be
at least fifteen minutes before help came. She slammed the phone down on
the car seat in frustration, but then thought to call her office to apologize to
Aidan and reschedule the next two in case she was an hour late. She dialed
her office number, and nothing happened. She tried again and the phone
emitted a plaintive bleep, signifying the juice was gone; the battery had died.

She had no charger in the car.

Over an hour later, she rushed into her office waiting room, hot and dust blown. Aidan was there of course, reading an old Men's Health magazine promising spectacular abs. There was a cardboard Starbucks container next to him with two tall cups.

"Aidan," she said, the last person she wished to see before she could get into the bathroom and fix her face and brush her hair. "I'm so sorry. It was an emergency. Give me a minute." He nodded and smiled his smile, both knowing and childlike.

Minutes later, Sylvia settled down across from Aidan in her office. She refused his offer of the coffee he'd brought for her, now cold. He, too, may have dressed with care: a blue dress shirt, tight black jeans, and boat shoes without socks. No watch, no rings, no piercings. In their two prior sessions, she'd learned that he had a college degree in mathematics from USC.

"Maybe we should start where we left off after our last session," she said.

"Not about my letter to you?"

"We'll get to that. But for now, there's more to talk about why the cutting."

"That's why I'm here."

"Not to stop it?"

"It seems harmless enough. So far." He rolled up his sleeves. On each arm light welts ran up his forearms like a tattoo of flowerless stems. They emerged from what appeared like a small pot—deeper slashes crisscrossing both wrists.

"Doesn't look so harmless to me. You see a doctor for that?" No obvious cuts had been added since his last visit.

"Use Polysporin. My dad's a doctor. Not serious if it doesn't get infected."

His father was a new subject. "You discussed cutting with your father?"

"God, no."

"Why not?"

"He's a neurosurgeon. Cuts people's brains open."

There were many directions Sylvia could take from here. "Interesting."

"Evan from work noticed it," Aidan said. "He's done it too, as a teenager. Said he did it to hurt himself. But I don't want to hurt myself. Just need to do it sometimes."

"When are the sometimes?" she asked.

"When I'm alone with too much time on my hands," he answered. As if he'd rehearsed for her.

"I thought that's when boys, excuse me, men masturbated," she said, surprising herself. Talk about compulsion. Why did she let the direction of her thoughts drive his session? Someone's insurance company was paying good money for her professionalism.

Aidan blushed. "That too."

They spent the next half hour exploring Aidan's self-image, his feelings about his job, and his relationship with his father. There was time enough remaining. Sylvia penciled an arrow heading for a question mark in her notebook. She heard the susurrus of late morning traffic.

"Maybe now we should talk about your letter." She reached for the cold coffee on the end table next to Aidan and took a sip.

"If you like."

Sylvia hesitated. It shouldn't be about what she liked. It should be about what he needed. But what if she was what he needed, and… She brushed away the sense of a cobweb prickling her.

Aidan rose from his chair and wiped the back of her neck, his hand like a caress.

She startled. "What…"

"A bug. Crawled up your shoulder. Sorry," he said.

Was it? Was he? He didn't look sorry. She took a breath. Where were they? "Your letter? It was…nice," she said. "And it shows you thought about boundaries between patients and therapists." Back on firm ground. "You know about transference, I assume?"

Aidan kept his eyes on her with unwavering male attention. He recited from memory: "In a therapy context, transference refers to redirection of a patient's feelings for a significant person to the therapist. It is often manifested as an erotic attraction towards a therapist."

She couldn't resist being charmed. "That's very impressive."

"Just Wikipedia, not the original sources."

"Aidan. Do you think your letter represents transference?"

"Of course it does. As do many feelings when getting to know someone."

Sylvia picked up the pencil and made a smiley face in her notebook. But she needed to be serious. "So who do you think of when you think about me?"

"Diana."

"Is she a friend, a family member?"

"Neither. A goddess." Aidan's voice remained emotionless, but with his eyes, his dark eyes, he appeared as if he were systematically appreciating her face, hair, clothes, breasts, waist, thighs, calves, and ankles, and even her Ferragamos that she'd scuffed on the gravel by the side of the freeway. She perspired lightly.

"Help me out here," she said. "Is this Diana an old girlfriend? Tell me about her."

"No. A real goddess. Artemis in Greek. The pale moon goddess of chastity and the chase. She could tame wild animals. Patroness of Wiccans."

Chastity? Wiccans? He was wasting their time, playing with her. "I guess that will give us more than enough to talk about next time."

Aidan looked up at her with an expression of irritated hurt, as if she were mocking him. Perhaps she was. The confused little pisher. Why hadn't he picked her as Hero to his Leander, Ariadne, or Venus, instead of the cold huntress, Diana?

"That's our hour, Aidan. I think we've made some progress today." A boilerplate closer. So what if she liked a young man who liked her.

He stood to leave, stretched his arms out to his side, and rolled his neck. She repressed the impulse to leap out of her chair and into his arms, press her cheek against his chest, smell his bare skin. Instead she said, "I have a suggestion. Why don't you write me another letter, and we can talk about it at our next appointment?"

"Another? I thought you were mad at me today. The talk about boundaries. I thought maybe I overstepped." He looked hopeful.

"Just write down whatever you're feeling during the week. It may open up some opportunities." The last was wrong. Just slipped out. Sylvia bit her lip. Aidan stumbled on the throw rug as he left her office.

The following week, Aidan didn't show for his appointment. He didn't call, even though she waited in the office for over half an hour, the last appointment of the day, his. At his previous visit, she should have run the screen for suicide risk.

"Sylvia!" Her Sunday walk to the beach had taken her by the kiosks selling art and handicrafts along Shoreline Drive. Aidan waved at her and came up hurriedly. "My fault. Major apology. Missing our last appointment."

Despite herself, Sylvia felt pleasure at his "our" rather than "my." But he'd missed the appointment and not called.

"Hi, Aidan," she said. "I was kind of worried." Then coolly, "I'm sorry but I'll have to charge you." He waved it away. One hundred and fifty dollars. A thing of no importance to him. On a salary from Kinkos. Hell, she was still living close to the bone.

He made inconsequential excuses. She hardly listened. She wasn't on the clock. It was a crisp fall day. She craved the sunshine that she missed in the cocoon of her office. Pleasant to stroll. Now and again his hand brushed hers.

Aidan also painted. "A lot of schlock," he said, referring to many of the paintings displayed by the hopeful artists along their way. Even she knew that. But Aidan had an eye.

"Look at the light in her eyes," he said as he pointed to an artfully draped nude. "A deft touch. Talented, but could use more imagination."

No problem for Sylvia. She imagined herself as the nude, Aidan's eyes lighting up when he entered the room where she reclined.

They stopped at a tent while Sylvia picked up a brochure for an upcoming fundraiser for breast cancer. She chatted with the blonde cancer survivor staffing the tent, consciously keeping her eyes on the blonde's appealing face. The fundraiser was in Montecito at the house of a former patient, Todd, who now was CFO of a major biotech firm. It would be fun but the 250-dollar ticket was too rich for her. As she turned away, she bumped into Todd himself, who greeted her warmly and offered her and Aidan two free tickets. Aidan fidgeted at her side like Sam at the checkout in Lucky's. "Look," he said. "It's so nice." He reached for her hand. The first time he'd held any part of her. "But I really have to run." She still held Todd's two tickets in her hand. No mention of rescheduling, he was gone.

Would she ever understand men? How could she counsel couples, when obviously most women were tied to losers who they dragged to therapy? She shrugged and took some deep breaths. One good thing about fantasies: no strings.

"Mom! It's just algebra and a little trig. Try and pay attention."

At the kitchen table in their bungalow, Sylvia helped Sam with his homework. He'd caught her daydreaming. It had been a long day. She'd seen whiny couples in back-to-back sessions, and wanted to smack them upside the head, tell them to suck it up and not be such crybabies. The washing machine was leaping all over the garage, banging around on the spin cycle, probably needing an expensive repair. Earlier that day, about lunchtime, Sam had called her saying she'd sent him to school with a paper bag containing no lunch, just a high-heeled shoe left in a bag by the sink, one that she'd torn at Todd's Montecito fundraiser. So for supper, Sam and Sylvia shared his tuna fish sandwich from the other paper bag while she suffered Sam's labeling her Mother of the Year. Sam, who she hoped she hadn't parentalized, knew enough not to give her crap at certain times of the month. The rich-rich guests at the fundraiser should try to raise an adolescent boy on their own and fight for some trickle-down support from an archetypical Deadbeat Dad.

"So, if it's that easy, maybe you can solve the next equation without using your iPad, the way we did it back in the day, kiddo."

Sam scribbled away with his pencil while she looked at the Santa Barbara Times. Near the bottom of the front page was a small picture of a scowling Aidan. "Life Saved Twice" was the headline. Aidan Tower stood beside an older woman, Jill Madson, who had her arm around him. She was one of the Dragon Boat ladies, cancer survivors who paddled a large Polynesian canoe to stay in shape.

Sylvia read that Aidan, a rower in college, was their manager and trainer. Jill had tumbled overboard from shocked surprise when a curious porpoise had surfaced next to their boat. Aidan, the coxswain—Sylvia smiled at the term—had jumped in the ocean and pulled Jill back into the boat. Aidan. Smart, good-looking, and now a hero. He had called during the week, and she knew that he was on her calendar for the next day.

Squirreling away on his homework, Sam was the one good thing from a busted marriage. She tousled Sam's blond hair. "Don't forget to use your Retin-A tonight," she said, noting a blooming pimple on his chin. After brushing her teeth she stuck her head back in the kitchen and said, "If you weren't so adorable, I wouldn't nag you so much," and got the smile from him that made her life livable. He was what love was, the kind associated with oxytocin, not estrogen.

In the morning, she told Sam she might be late-late. Supper was in the fridge ready to be microwaved. She dressed hurriedly, not thinking about what she pulled out of the closet. She had a hair appointment before her first patient. As an afterthought, she moved her face through a light mist of Arpège. Rushing out the door, she spotted the letter along with some junk mail that had been dropped through the mail slot and kicked aside from yesterday.

Hello Sylvia,

Well, what to say? It's been a day at work—the usual squabbles between Laura and Jane, with me in the middle. Laura's a jerk, doesn't know what's going on in her own department. But today she really lost it, yelled at the only other guy in our department, and true, he is a little dim. He'd emailed copies of all the personnel files from the R&D folks to the head of marketing by mistake. R&D people hate Marketing. Laura went berserk. She made me get a note from him that he'd done it, and I had to countersign it. All of us in personnel looked like complete fuckups.

Sylvia scanned the rest of the three-page letter. Where was the admiration, or at least the interest of the first letter? The letter ended with:

I think the week started badly when nobody remembered my birthday except Ellie. She works in the advertising dept. It was really nice of her. She even took me out to lunch and ordered up a cupcake with a candle…

Sylvia could have looked on the entry form that Aidan had filled out. She could have remembered his birthday. Brought up useful emotions. She jammed the letter deep in her purse to add to Aidan's file.

Later, surrounded by the comfort of her office, Sylvia felt more herself. While Aidan settled across from her, she arranged a framed picture on the side table. It was of a grinning Sam holding his birthday present, a new surfboard. He and Sylvia had arms around each other.

"Let's roam a little farther afield today, Aidan. We've talked about the cutting. About psychological mechanisms. Now, I wonder if you could tell me a little more about how you became Aidan."

"Sure," the always willing Aidan said. "Father's an asshole. No brothers. One sister in San Francisco with four kids. No other close family. Schools. Sports. College. Started grad school. Like everyone."

Her women patients would have filled a month's worth of sessions with what he'd just told her. Silence filled the room.

"And then?" she asked, finally.

"Just kind of stopped."

"More about that?"

"Mom died. Cancer."

Sylvia waited. Aidan kept looking at her feet. "Do you feel like saying more?"

"Mom was great. She kept me safe."

Then it came out in bursts. He was almost crying. "Like you. Same red hair. Same smile."

Sylvia twiddled her pencil and noticed a pimple to the right of Aidan's nose. She stifled a huge yawn. Sylvia was no longer Venus, not even Diana, she was his mom. She rubbed her eyes, her face. Aidan now seemed somewhat scruffy, the same species as her son.

Aidan couldn't keep his mom safe. Guilt. Pop mostly absent. Unresolved Oedipal feelings. Cutting. Sylvia pulled down her skirt, wrapped her sweater close. Made a note on her pad. She could help this kid.

"Tell me more. Sounds as if I would have liked her." Sylvia now knew where she was going, to a *shiva* for a dead mother.

Brittany Ackerman is a writer from Riverdale, New York. She teaches Archetypal Psychology at AMDA College and Conservatory of the Performing Arts in Hollywood, CA. Her work has been featured in *The Los Angeles Review, No Tokens, Hobart, Cosmonauts Ave, Fiction Southeast*, and more. She currently lives in Los Angeles, California with her first collection of essays entitled *The Perpetual Motion Machine* out with Red Hen Press.

Rachel Barton is a poet, writing coach, and editor. She is a member of the *Calyx* Editorial Collective, reads for *Cloudbank*, and edits her own *Willawaw Journal*. Find her poems in *Oregon English Journal, Hubbub, Whale Road Review, Mom Egg Review*, and elsewhere. Her chapbook, *Out of the Woods*, was released in 2017. *Happiness Comes* was released from Dancing Girl Press in 2018. Both are available on her website, rachelbartonwriter. com.

Jon Bennett has taught high school English for nine years, the last three in California. His debut novel, *Reading Blue Devils*, was published in February of 2018. His wife, Nicole, and daughter, Charlotte, are his greatest inspirations and distractions.

Jo-Anne Cappeluti has poems recently appearing in *Lindenwood Review, Spiritus*, and *Blue Unicorn*. She continues in retirement to explore her passion for poetry: both in writing about poets such as W.H. Auden and John Keats and in writing poetry. She earned her PhD in English from the University of California at Riverside.

Jim Cole writes overlooking the Russian River in the town of Duncans Mills, California. A recipient of the 2017 PEN/Robert J. Dau Short Story Prize for Emerging Writers, his stories have appeared in various journals, including *The Summerset Review, Crack the Spine*, and T*he Esthetic Apostle*. He has an MFA from the University of San Francisco, where he was nominated for the AWP Intro Journals Project for his novel *ffrrfr*.

Alexis Rhone Fancher is published in *Best American Poetry, Rattle, Hobart, Verse Daily, Plume, Tinderbox, Cleaver, Diode, Duende*, and elsewhere. Her books include: *How I Lost My Virginity to Michael Cohen...*, *State of Grace: The Joshua Elegies, Enter Here, Junkie Wife*, and *The Dead Kid Poems*. Her latest, *EROTIC: New & Selected*, publishes in 2020 from *New York Quarterly*. Her photographs are published worldwide. A multiple Pushcart Prize nominee, Alexis is poetry editor of *Cultural Weekly*. www.alexisrhonefancher.com

Savanna Ferguson's work focuses on science, natural history, and the environment, and has been featured in *La.Lit* magazine, the *San Francisco Chronicle*, and at *F&B: Voices from the Kitchen*. She lives in Berkeley but can often be found leading tours at the San Francisco Botanical Garden. She is currently working on a collection of linked essays about how human vices have shaped our relationship with different species over the centuries.

Thomas Hedt lives northern California. He has been involved in conservation for a few decades and took up poetry while hiking in the inter-coastal range. He enjoys roasting coffee, and routinely looks for excuses to see the sunset over the Pacific. Previous work has been published in *The Sacramento Voices*, the *Tule Review*, and the *Sijo International Journal of Poetry and Song*.

Phillip Hurst lives and writes in Oregon. He's spent the last decade bartending and teaching throughout the American West.

Bronwyn Mauldin is the author of the novel *Love Songs of the Revolution* and the short story collection *The Streetwise Cycle*. Her short fiction has been published by *Akashic Books*, *The Coffin Factory*, *CutBank*, *Literature for Life*, and others. She has been a writer in residence at both Mesa Verde National Park and Denali National Park. She's also creator of the *Democracy Series* zine collection.

Barbara McClure has taught English and creative writing at San Francisco State and Santa Rosa Junior College and has been living in the Bay Area for years. Three years ago, her my husband and her built a Montana home overlooking the Madison River where they now spend their summers writing and fly fishing. "Memory" is part of a collection she's currently working on, titled *The Wichita Stories*.

Leah Mueller is the author of two chapbooks and four books. Her next two books, "Death and Heartbreak" and "Misguided Behavior, Tales of Poor Life Choices" will be published in 2019 by Weasel Press and Czykmate Press. Leah's work appears in *Blunderbuss*, *The Spectacle*, *Outlook Springs*, *Atticus Review*, *Your Impossible Voice*, and elsewhere.

Simon Nagel's short fiction has appeared in *The Glasgow Review of Books*, *Fairlight Books* online, and *Flash Fiction Magazine*. He has written artificial intelligence for Samsung and the pilot episode of The Future with Dan Kaufman for CNBC. Simon was the inaugural winner of The Hasty Pudding Institute Screenwriting Fellowship. He is currently writing his first novel.

Brendan Praniewicz resides in San Diego, California. He teaches English and Creative Writing at local community colleges. Aside from writing, he enjoys photography and performing stand-up comedy. His poems and stories have been published in *Races Y Mas*, *Driftwood Press*, *Tiny Seed Journal*, and *Watershed Press*.

Edythe Schwartz is the author of "A Palette of Leaves," Mayapple Press, and "Exposure," Finishing Line Press. Her work appears widely in journals including *The Southern Review*, *Poet Lore*, *Spillway*, *Faultline*, and *Cave Wall*, among others. Besides working with words, she makes visual art with paint, paper, fiber, and assorted recycled materials.

Claire Scott is an award-winning poet who has received multiple Pushcart Prize nominations. Her work has been accepted by the *Atlanta Review*, *Bellevue Literary Review*, *New Ohio Review*, *Enizagam*, and *Healing Muse* among others. Claire is the author of Waiting to be Called and Until I Couldn't. She is the co-author of Unfolding in Light: A Sisters' Journey in Photography and Poetry.

Frank Scozzari, a Pushcart Prize nominee, resides in Nipomo, a small town on the California central coast. He is an avid traveler and once climbed Mt. Kilimanjaro, the highest point in Africa. His award-winning short stories have appeared in numerous literary magazines including *The Emerson Review*, *Berkeley Fiction Review*, *Tampa Review*, *Pacific Review*, *Minetta Review*, *Reed Magazine*, *Worcester Review*, *Roanoke Review*, and *War Literature & the Arts*, and have been featured in literary theater.

Xavier Stone earned his MA in English from Missouri State University in 2013. He was awarded a Durwood fellowship at University of Missouri-Kansas City, where he received his MFA in Creative Writing and Media Arts in 2015. He lives in Portland, OR.

H. William Taeusch graduated from Harvard College where he transferred from a brutal Physics 1 into Physics for English majors after he received his acceptance to medical school. More recently he completed an MA from the excellent Shaindy Rudoff Program in Creative Writing at Bar-Ilan University in Israel. Two of the journals that published his stories are now defunct. He's at work on a series of novels in which Eli Kurz MD breaks down if not bad. He's related to Skyler White by ex-marriage. A chapter from one of the novels was recently anthologized in ISRAEL SHORT STORIES. He lives in God's country, California and Israel.

J. T. Townley has published in *Harvard Review, The Kenyon Review, The Threepenny Review*, and other magazines and journals. His stories have been nominated for the Pushcart Prize and Best of the Net award. He holds an MFA in Creative Writing from the University of British Columbia and an MPhil in English from Oxford University. To learn more, visit jttownley.com.

Jason Wallace is a short story writer who lives in Northern California. He enjoys fishing, lifting weights, and racing flat track motorcycles.

Cedric Yamanaka is the author of *In Good Company*, a collection of short stories. He is a recipient of the Helen Deutsch Fellowship for Creative Writing from Boston University, the Ernest Hemingway Memorial Award for Creative Writing from the University of Hawaii, and the Cades Award for Literature. He is currently working on a novel.

Andrena Zawinski's poetry has received accolades for lyricism, form, spirituality, social concern. Her collections are *Landings, Something About* (PEN Oakland Award), and *Traveling in Reflected Light* (Kenneth Patchen Poetry Prize). She also compiled and edited *Turning a Train of Thought Upside Down: An Anthology of Women's Poetry*. Long time teacher of writing and feminist, she is Features Editor at *PoetryMagazine.com* and runs the San Francisco Bay Area Women's Poetry Salon.

www.ingramcontent.com/pod-product-compliance
Lightning Source LLC
Chambersburg PA
CBHW031835170626
46807CB00004B/1476